hors d'oeuvre etc.

by coralie castle and barbara lawrence

drawings by karen lynch

101 productions
san francisco
1973

Sixth Printing, March 1980

Library of Congress Catalog Card Number 73-81084

Distributed to the Book Trade in the United States of America
by Charles Scribner's Sons, New York

PUBLISHED BY 101 PRODUCTIONS
834 Mission Street
San Francisco, California 94103

contents

Basics: Sauces, Stocks, Garnitures and Hints 5

Breads, Spreads, Sandwiches and Canapes 21

Appetizers: Cold, Hot and Dips 45

Molds, Patés, Terrines and Galantines 70

Soups and Stoppers 86

Pastries, Phyllo, Quiches and Tarts 100

Chafing Dish Cookery 121

Fireside, Firepot, Fondue and Barbecue 132

Buffets, Chinese Buffet and Buffet Desserts 146

Glossary 185

Index 187

Biographical Data 192

introduction

For most people, the term "hors d'oeuvre" conjures up visions of tasty morsels served at cocktail parties. As one of the best-known French expressions in the English language, its grammatical status is changing from a phrase meaning "outside the work (main meal)" to a noun to which an "s" may be added to designate more than one morsel.

For this reason "Hors d'Oeuvre" alone is an inadequate title for a book that covers all sorts of delightful viands outside the main meal for every kind of entertaining. Hence, the "Etc."

History records the enjoyment of appetizers as far back as 3000 B.C. in Japan. The Mandarins of ancient China took pride in over 1000 *ti wei ping*. Athenians enjoyed *dolmas* in 350 B.C. In early Rome *gustotio* meant over fifty "tasters." That epitome of extravagance, Emperor Lucullus, thought nothing of spending thousands to obtain obscure eggs, spices, herbs—even peacock tongues —for just one meal. In Sybaris only morsels were served at drinking bouts that lasted for days.

Word-coiners have long been preoccupied with much more than mere breakfast, luncheon and dinner. There have been bevers and tiffins; collops, dollops and gobbets; dibs and dabs; minims, mites and minikins; canapes, kickshaws and cates; sippets, trifles and tidbits. Today one finds *acepipes* in Portugal, *antipasto* in Italy, *maza* in Syria, *mezeler* in Turkey, *zakuska* in Russia, and endless other small foods.

What might be called the "in-between meal" can be just as important, just as enjoyable, just as challenging as an elaborate dinner. There are fascinating ways of entertaining, of pleasing the eye and palate with thoughtfully prepared food at an extra or substitute meal, before or after dinner, for a gala celebration or intimate soirée, with but a few pretty plates of dainty morsels or an elaborate array of platter spectaculars. Nibbling, sipping and munching with friends call for the very finest in the fragile art of food.

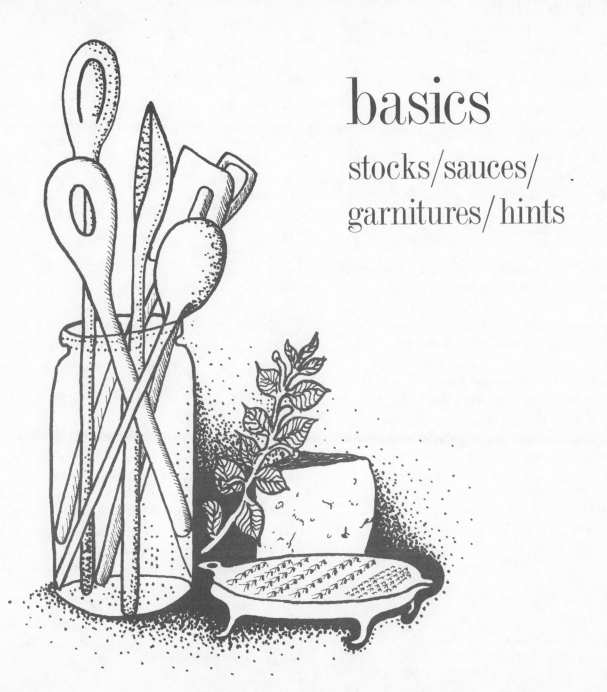

basics

stocks/sauces/
garnitures/hints

basics: sauces

MAYONNAISE
(Hand Method)

3 egg yolks, room temperature
1-1/2 to 2 tablespoons lemon juice or
    cider vinegar or tarragon vinegar
1/2 teaspoon salt
1/4 teaspoon each paprika and white pepper
1-1/2 to 2 cups salad oil or olive oil
2 tablespoons boiling water

In wooden bowl or warmed pottery bowl beat the yolks with a wooden spoon until thickened. Beat in 1 tablespoon of the lemon juice or vinegar and the seasonings. Continuing to beat *constantly*, in a thin steady stream pour in 1/2 cup of the oil. Little by little beat in the rest of oil, adding the rest of the lemon juice or vinegar alternately. Adjust seasonings and gradually beat in boiling water. Cover and refrigerate. If mayonnaise curdles, start with another egg yolk and gradually beat in curdled mayonnaise and then more oil. Never use more than 3/4 cup oil for each egg yolk. This mayonnaise may also be made in an electric mixer set on lowest speed.
Makes approximately 2-1/4 cups

MAYONNAISE
(Blender Method)

1 egg
2 tablespoons lemon juice or cider vinegar or
    tarragon vinegar
1/2 teaspoon salt
1/4 teaspoon paprika
1/2 teaspoon minced garlic (optional)
1/4 teaspoon dry mustard (optional)
1 cup salad oil or olive oil

Place egg, lemon juice or vinegar, seasonings and 1/4 cup of the oil in container of blender. Blend on low speed 5 or 6 seconds. In a steady slow stream pour in remaining oil. When incorporated, blend on high speed 4 or 5 seconds. Adjust seasonings, cover and refrigerate.
Makes approximately 1-1/4 cups

Variations
• Herb Mayonnaise: When blending egg add the garlic and 1/4 cup mixed fresh herbs.
• Watercress mayonnaise: to basic mayonnaise add 1 cup chopped watercress.
• Mustard mayonnaise: to basic mayonnaise add Dijon-style or dry mustard to taste.
• Caper mayonnaise: to basic mayonnaise add minced parsley and capers to taste.
• Curry mayonnaise: to basic mayonnaise made with lemon juice add curry powder to taste.
• Aioli: to basic mayonnaise made with lemon juice add lots of garlic.

HOLLANDAISE
(Blender Method)

1/2 pound butter
4 egg yolks
2 tablespoons lemon juice
1/2 teaspoon salt
1/4 teaspoon each paprika and freshly grated
    lemon peel (optional)
1/8 teaspoon white pepper
2 drops Tabasco

Cut butter into pieces and melt until hot but not brown. Place all other ingredients in blender. On low speed blend 2 or 3 seconds. In steady thin stream pour in heated butter. Adjust seasonings and serve immediately.
Makes approximately 1-1/4 cups

Note: If it is necessary to hold sauce for a short time put container in hot water 2 inches up the sides. Refrigerate leftover sauce in covered container up to 4 days. Sauce does not reheat without curdling but if put on hot foods it will melt sufficiently. One tablespoon orange juice may be substituted for 1 tablespoon of the lemon juice, in which case use grated orange peel instead of lemon peel.

BÉARNAISE

1/4 cup each wine vinegar and dry white wine
1 tablespoon minced white of green onion
1/4 teaspoon minced garlic
2 teaspoons each minced tarragon and parsley
1/8 teaspoon pepper
1/16 teaspoon cayenne pepper
2 tablespoons tomato purée (optional)
1-1/4 cups hollandaise, previous recipe,
    without lemon juice

Combine all ingredients except tomato purée. Bring to boil and cook until reduced to 2 tablespoons. Use instead of lemon juice in hollandaise sauce. Add tomato purée if desired and adjust seasonings to taste.
Makes approximately 1-1/4 cups

basics: sauces

MOUSSELINE

3/4 cup hollandaise sauce
1/4 cup heavy cream, whipped
1/2 teaspoon lemon juice
1/4 cup homemade mayonnaise
1/8 teaspoon nutmeg
salt and pepper to taste

Combine ingredients.
Makes approximately 1-1/2 cups

VELOUTÉ SAUCE

4 tablespoons butter
1/2 cup chopped onion
1/4 cup chopped parsley
1/4 cup flour
1 cup each half-and-half and meat,
    poultry or fish stock
1/2 teaspoon salt
1/4 teaspoon each white pepper and
    thyme or nutmeg

Melt butter until bubbly and sauté onion and parsley until soft but not browned. Sprinkle with flour, cook and stir 3 minutes. Slowly add half-and-half and stock, stir until thick and then continue cooking, stirring often, 15 minutes. Strain and add seasonings. Adjust and thin with more half-and-half or stock if necessary.
Makes 2 cups

MORNAY SAUCE

2 cups velouté sauce, heated
3 egg yolks, beaten
1/4 cup cream or stock
3 tablespoons each grated Gruyère and
    Parmesan cheese
2 tablespoons butter

Beat yolks with a little hot sauce and return to rest of sauce with stock and cheeses. Cook and stir without boiling until thickened. Just before serving add butter and swirl to melt.
Makes approximately 2-1/4 cups

CURRY SAUCE

1/2 recipe velouté sauce made with beef stock
1 to 2 teaspoons curry powder
1 tablespoon minced chives

Combine ingredients and adjust to taste.

WHISKEY SAUCE

1/4 pound butter, melted
2 tablespoons whiskey
3 tablespoons minced chives and/or parsley
2 teaspoons Worcestershire sauce

Combine and heat ingredients; adjust to taste.

BORDELAISE SAUCE

Brown Sauce
1-1/2 tablespoons each clarified butter* and flour
1-1/2 cups strong beef broth
1/2 cup chopped onion
1 clove garlic, halved
1 small bay leaf
1/2 teaspoon each salt and paprika
1/4 teaspoon pepper
1/4 cup sherry (optional)
1/4 cup tomato purée (optional)

*See glossary

Melt butter until bubbly, sprinkle with flour and cook, stirring often, until color of brown wrapping paper. Use heavy skillet so roux does not scorch. Gradually blend in broth; cook and stir until thickened. Add onion, garlic, seasonings and sherry. Cook until reduced to 1 cup. Strain and add tomato purée if desired.
2 shallots, minced
1/2 cup red wine
1 cup brown sauce
2 tablespoons minced marrow
3 tablespoons minced parsley

Cook shallots and wine until reduced to 1/3 cup. Add brown sauce and boil gently 10 minutes. Just before serving add marrow and parsley.

CHUTNEY SAUCE

Mix 2 parts chopped chutney to 1 part sugar. Heat until syrupy and season to taste with lemon juice.

HERB SAUCE

1/4 pound butter
2 tablespoons each minced parsley and chives
1/2 teaspoon each minced thyme,
    rosemary and basil
1 tablespoon grated onion
salt and pepper

Melt butter with herbs and onion. Adjust with salt and pepper to taste.

basics: sauces

ANCHOVY SAUCE

3/4 cup olive oil
1 or 2 2-ounce cans anchovy fillets, mashed
1/3 cup wine vinegar
1/2 to 1 teaspoon pressed garlic
3 tablespoons minced parsley
1 teaspoon minced basil

Combine ingredients and heat. Adjust to taste.

TOMATO SAUCE

1/3 cup chopped onions
1/4 cup each chopped celery and parsley
2 tablespoons minced green pepper (optional)
1 teaspoon minced garlic
2 tablespoons butter
1 tablespoon olive oil
4 large ripe tomatoes, peeled, seeded and chopped
6 tarragon leaves, minced
1/2 teaspoon each sugar and salt
1/4 teaspoon pepper
1 teaspoon each butter and flour

Sauté vegetables and garlic in butter and oil, covered, until soft. Add tomatoes, tarragon and seasonings. Cook, uncovered, until reduced to 1-3/4 cups, stirring occasionally. Purée in blender and reheat with a paste of 1 teaspoon each butter and flour. Cook and stir 5 minutes; adjust seasonings.
Makes approximately 1-1/2 cups

VINAIGRETTE SAUCE

3/4 cup garlic olive oil*
1/3 cup tarragon or cider vinegar
2 tablespoons each finely minced celery,
    carrot and parsley
1 tablespoon each minced chervil,
    minced chives and grated onion
2 teaspoons each finely minced green
    pepper and capers (optional)
1/2 teaspoon salt
1/4 teaspoon each dry mustard and pepper
1 sieved hard-cooked egg (optional)

*See glossary

Combine all ingredients except egg. Chill several hours and just before serving add egg. Good on fish, meat, vegetable salads.
Makes about 1-1/2 cups

HORSERADISH SAUCE

1/2 cup sour cream
2 tablespoons prepared horseradish
1/2 teaspoon sugar
1 small tart apple, pared and grated
1 to 2 teaspoons lemon juice
1/2 teaspoon grated lemon rind
1/8 teaspoon cayenne pepper

Blend ingredients and adjust to taste. Refrigerate several hours.
Makes 3/4 cup

SOUR CREAM DILL SAUCE

1/2 pint sour cream
2 tablespoons fresh minced dill weed
1 teaspoon sugar
1/4 teaspoon each salt and white pepper

Combine ingredients and adjust to taste. Refrigerate.

BOILED DRESSING OR CREAM DRESSING

1 egg, beaten
1 egg yolk
1/2 cup each salad oil and heavy cream
1/4 cup white wine vinegar, plain or with herbs
1 teaspoon sugar
1/2 teaspoon salt
1/4 teaspoon each white pepper and paprika
1/4 teaspoon dry mustard (optional)

In top of double boiler beat all ingredients until well blended. Cook over hot water (not boiling), stirring often until thickened. Mixture should coat wooden spoon when spoon is tipped. Strain, cool, cover and chill.
Makes 1-1/2 cups

FRENCH DRESSING

2/3 cup olive or salad oil
1/4 cup cider vinegar or lemon juice
1 teaspoon salt
1/2 teaspoon pepper
chopped pimiento
1 to 2 tablespoons grated Parmesan or
    Romano cheese
chopped or sieved hard-cooked egg
1 tablespoon crumbled bacon
chopped anchovies or anchovy paste

Combine oil, vinegar, salt and pepper. Add choice of remaining ingredients depending upon vegetable or salad being served. Adjust seasonings and chill. Shake well before using.
Makes approximately 1 cup

YOGHURT SAUCE

1 cup yoghurt
2 tablespoons each minced mint and lemon juice
1 teaspoon finely minced garlic

Combine ingredients and adjust to taste. Refrigerate.

basics: sauces

MUSHROOM DUXELLE

1/4 cup finely minced green onions and tops
4 tablespoons butter
1/2 pound mushrooms, finely minced
1/4 teaspoon each salt, oregano and pepper
1/2 teaspoon lemon juice
2 tablespoons flour
1 cup heavy cream
2 tablespoons minced parsley
1 tablespoon minced chives
3 to 4 drops Tabasco

Sauté onions in butter 3 minutes; add mushrooms, seasonings and lemon juice. Cook, stirring often, until moisture is almost evaporated, depending upon freshness of mushrooms. Sprinkle with flour and cook and stir 3 minutes. Gradually add cream and cook and stir until thickened. Add parsley, chives and Tabasco. Adjust seasonings and cool. May be frozen in small jars up to 1 month.
Makes 1-1/2 cups

TOMATO-HAM DUXELLE

3 large ripe tomatoes, peeled, seeded,
    chopped and drained
1/4 cup finely minced green onions and tops
1 teaspoon minced garlic
1/4 pound mushrooms, finely minced
3/4 cup finely minced ham
1/4 teaspoon each salt, pepper and oregano
3 tablespoons finely minced parsley
3 to 4 drops Tabasco
3 egg yolks, beaten

Cook tomatoes, onions, garlic, mushrooms, ham and seasonings until mushrooms are tender and moisture has evaporated. Add parsley and Tabasco and adjust to taste. Beat 1 cup of mixture into egg yolks and return to rest of mixture, beating constantly. Cook and stir over medium heat until thickened. Do not boil. Cool. May be frozen in small jars up to 1 month.
Makes approximately 1-1/2 cups

POULTRY/GAME/MEAT STOCK

To every pound fresh or leftover bones add 1 quart water (for brown stock brown fresh bones in oven). Add fresh and leftover vegetables, vegetable scrapings, other scraps and water in which vegetables have been cooked. (For an unusual stock flavor add water in which artichokes have been cooked. Especially good with lamb stock.) Strengthen with blanched and rinsed pigs' feet, marrow bones and/or knuckle bones and with herbs and seasonings. Bring to gentle boil, skim off any scum that rises to the top, cover and simmer 2 to 4 hours. Strain, jar, cool, cover and refrigerate. If not using within 10 days, bring back to boil and re-jar. (Fat on top serves as a seal.) If freezing, leave 1 inch air space, store up to 3 months and bring back to boil before using.

To improve flavor
• To 1 quart poultry, lamb, veal or pork stock add 1/4 cup each minced carrot, onion, mushroom stems (optional) and celery and tops, 1 small bay leaf, 3 sprigs parsley and 1/4 teaspoon each thyme, turmeric and savory. Simmer 1-1/2 hours and strain.
• For 1 quart beef stock follow above directions. Omit turmeric and add 1/2 cup dry red or white wine and 1 tablespoon tomato paste (optional).

VEGETABLE STOCK

To 1 quart water and/or water in which vegetables have been cooked (or part tomato juice) add 3 cups chopped vegetables, 1 cup chopped parsley and other herbs and seasonings of choice. Proceed as for meat stock.

FISH STOCK

To every pound fish heads, bones and trimmings add 1 quart water, 3/4 cup dry white wine, 1/2 cup each sliced celery (and tops), onions and carrots, 6 parsley sprigs, 3 thyme sprigs, 3 tarragon leaves or 1 bay leaf, 8 peppercorns and 1/2 teaspoon salt. Proceed as for meat stock but cook only 30 minutes. To improve flavor cook 1 quart fish stock down to 3 cups or add bottled clam juice.

TO CLARIFY STOCK

Bring 3 cups to boil, add 1 slightly beaten egg white and 1 crumbled egg shell, bring back to boil, add 2 teaspoons cold water and bring back to boil for 2 minutes. Remove from heat and let stand without stirring 20 minutes. Pour through strainer lined with double cheesecloth that has been rinsed in cold water.

basics: garnitures

GARNITURES

Choose garnishes that complement the food being served and include a variety of tastes, textures and colors. Technically garnitures should be edible, but do take liberties. Use ivy leaves as a base for large garnitures such as a tomato rose or lemon half or form a mound of pâté on a large ivy leaf. Tuck fresh chrysanthemums or daisies into the center of a ring mold or around a pâté mound. When working with garnishes a very sharp knife is a must.

VEGETABLE FLOWERS

- Notch carrots 1/4 inch deep lengthwise (5 or 6 cuts); slice thinly.
- Cut green maraschino cherries almost through in 8ths, spread open and place red maraschino cherry half in center.
- Partially cut a slice off stem end of tomato; place knife point under skin at that spot and start to peel in spiral fashion leaving peel attached to stem slice. Be careful the skin does not break. Band should be about 1/2 inch wide. Place stem slice on board and wind peel up and around to make a rose. When finished peeling the peel will be detached entirely from the tomato. Or cut tomato into 8ths within 1 inch of bottom. Peel back skin of each 8th about halfway down and curl to resemble rose.
- Cut slice off both ends of red radish; slash cuts from tip to stem on slight diagonal around radish about halfway down. Open petals and crisp in ice water. Or trim top of radish, leaving stem on. Slice one way and then the other almost through to stem. Crisp in ice water.
- Form caviar as bunch of tiny grapes with parsley leaf and stem.
- Pierce 3 or 4 cranberries on toothpick and tuck picks in bed of parsley with cranberries at different angles.
- Fashion daisies with petals of hard-cooked egg white and ripe olives and green-pepper stem; or cut petals from pineapple slices and make leaves and stems of green pepper. Place green maraschino cherry or sieved hard-cooked egg yolk in center.
- Frost mint leaves, grapes, violets: Beat egg whites until frothy, dip leaves into whites, then into sugar or powdered sugar; repeat until coated. Dry on cake rack.
- Arrange ripe olive halves in shape of grape cluster; place celery leaves to make stem.
- With vegetable peeler slice paper-thin strips from carrot. Trim to 3-inch lengths and curl ends with scissors blade (the same way you make a ribbon curl). Fasten 3 strips together with a toothpick in the center. Spread carrot ends apart and crisp in ice water. Place small ripe olive in center.
- Cut carrots lengthwise very thinly with vegetable slicer, wrap around finger and secure with toothpick. Crisp in ice water and remove pick.

basics: garnitures

FILLED GARNITURES

• Fill artichoke bottoms with chopped hard-cooked eggs and parsley.
• Stuff tomatoes or beets.
• Cut carrots into 2-inch lengths. With apple corer hollow out center. Fill with cream cheese or other filling.
• Stuff lichee nuts with cream cheese.
• Cut carrots into tiny strips and stuff into pitted ripe olives; or use celery or green pepper strips and top with tiny piece of pimiento.
• With apple corer hollow out center of cucumber or dill pickle. Stuff with cream cheese mixed with chopped nuts and minced parsley and chives. Slice and sprinkle with paprika.
• Halve small cucumber and cut and hollow out to make basket with handle. Fill with cream cheese spread or parsley.
• Heat olives in garlic olive oil and wrap in anchovy fillet.
• Cut yellow plum tomatoes 3/4ths way down into 3 parts. Pull apart to make cup and fill center with parsley and/or watercress.

FANS

• Slice small pickles into 5 or 6 strips almost to stem. Spread apart.
• Cut zucchini, carrots, green onions or celery ribs into 2-inch lengths. Cut lengthwise into thin shreds up to 1/2 inch of end. Crisp in ice water. Or cut from both ends, leaving 1/2 inch uncut in center.
• Trim ends of green onion, cut off all but 3 inches of tops and shred tops down to white. Crisp in ice water.

LEMONS, ORANGES AND LIMES

• Put half of a lemon or orange cut side down and punch holes all over it with an ice pick; poke stems of flowers into the holes until the base is completely covered.
• Place halves cut side down on board. Make notches all around to flute edge. Place cut side up and tuck a small parsley sprig in center.
• To shape a basket: Cut away wedges to leave a handle and scoop out pulp with grapefruit knife. Fill with parsley or mint sprigs.
• Or cut small slice from bottom so lemon will stand, peel top half, leaving short handles on opposite sides; scoop out pulp and top with sprig of mint, chervil or parsley.
• Notch fruit lengthwise 1/4 inch deep, slice thinly and tuck a leaf of parsley or watercress in center.
• Or halve fruit and dip in minced parsley. Sprinkle with paprika.
• Or notch after slicing.
• Make a slight cut into 1/4-inch slice of orange and twist to make cornucopia. Put black olive in center.

JELLIES FOR COATING AND GARNISHES

Soften gelatin specified in recipe in cold liquid and dissolve in hot liquid or over hot water. Pour a small amount into a chilled saucer to depth of 1/4 inch. Refrigerate 10 minutes to set. Break up with fork. Pieces should hold their shape. If too syrupy add more softened gelatin and repeat; if jelly is rubbery add more liquid.

• *Consommé jelly:* Heat 1 10-ounce can consommé and add 1 teaspoon gelatin softened in 2 tablespoons lemon juice or dry vermouth or other wine. Use according to recipe.
• *Madrilene jelly:* Heat 1 13-ounce can madrilene and add 1-1/2 teaspoons gelatin softened in 2 tablespoons liquid. Use according to recipe.
• *Tomato jelly:* Simmer 1-1/2 cups tomato juice, 4 slices of onion, 1 bay leaf, 2 whole cloves, 1 teaspoon sugar and 1/4 teaspoon oregano 10 to 15 minutes. Strain and add 1 envelope gelatin dissolved in 1/2 cup tomato juice. Use according to recipe.
• *Vegetable jelly:* Soften 1 envelope gelatin in 3 tablespoons cold water and dissolve in 1-1/2 cups hot rich poultry, meat, vegetable or other stock. Chill to partially set and stir in 1 tablespoon each finely minced celery and parsley, 1 teaspoon each finely minced green pepper and grated onion, and seasonings to taste. Use according to recipe.
• *Madeira jelly:* Bring to boil 5 cups chicken or beef broth, 2 chopped tomatoes, 1/4 cup chopped green onion, 1 teaspoon minced tarragon, 2 slightly beaten egg whites and the crumbled shells of 2 eggs. Simmer at low boil 3 minutes. Remove from heat and let stand 20 minutes. Line a colander with cheesecloth wrung out in cold water and strain broth. Add 2 envelopes gelatin softened in 1/4 cup or more Madeira and stir to dissolve.
• *Homemade stocks:* Strain and clarify stocks. Depending upon how gelatinous stock is, allow 1 envelope gelatin for 2 cups of stock for aspics or decoration cutouts; 1 envelope gelatin for each 1-1/2 cups of stock for lining molds or coating canapes and other foods.
• *Mayonnaise collée:* Soften 1 envelope gelatin in 1/4 cup water or meat, poultry or fish stock and dissolve over hot water. Blend in 1-1/2 cups homemade mayonnaise and adjust with salt and white pepper. Use as coating for molds, canapes, meat, fish or poultry, stuffed tomatoes, eggs, salads, mousses.

LINING CONTAINERS WITH ASPIC

Prepare aspic of your choice from the preceding jelly recipes. Place container in a large bowl of crushed ice. Pour coating jelly into form to make coating 1/8 to 1/4 inch thick, tipping form to coat entirely and evenly. If there is too much jelly in the bottom, scoop out with heated spoon. Chill to set. To decorate, if desired, dip chilled garnishes in coating jelly and arrange on aspic. Chill to set and fill with chilled mold mixture. Coat with another thin layer of jelly.

basics: garnitures

COATING FOODS WITH ASPIC

The following method can be used to coat canapes, meats, poultry, fish, terrines, molded aspics, garnishes, etc. Keep foods to be coated thoroughly chilled. Place them on the rack or platter in which they are to be served. Place small foods such as olives, egg slices, cherry tomatoes on wire mesh if they are to be coated separately. Prepare one of the preceding jellies for coating and place bowl of jelly over ice until syrupy. If jelly becomes too firm, heat briefly until again syrupy. Work with a small amount of jelly at a time so that jelly does not become cloudy from bits of food. Using a feather brush, spread a thin layer of the coating jelly over the food; chill to set and repeat until coating is 1/8 to 1/4 inch thick. For garnishes and small foods, use tweezers to dip them into the coating jelly. Decorate coated food with garnishes. Chill to set and finish with a thin coating of jelly.

ASPIC CUTOUTS FOR GARNITURES

Prepare 1 cup jelly for coating from the preceding recipes. Rinse a large shallow dish in cold water, pour in jelly to depth of approximately 1/4 inch. Refrigerate until firm and cut into shapes with tiny hors d'oeuvre cutters. Or cut into tiny cubes and mound around foods to be garnished.

EGG-ASPIC CUTOUTS FOR GARNITURES

Prepare 1 cup jelly for coating from the preceding recipes. Pour 1/4 cup jelly into 8-inch pie plate that has been rinsed in cold water. Refrigerate until firm. Purée yolks of 3 hard-cooked eggs and remaining jelly in blender and pour over aspic. Chill until firm and cut into shapes with tiny hors d'oeuvre cutters.

IDEAS FOR DECORATING ASPIC-LINED MOLDS OR ASPIC-COATED FOODS

Design, pattern and decorations depend upon shape, design and content of mold. Suggested decorations:
- Black olives cut in half or in thin strips.
- Pimientos cut in thin strips or small pieces.
- Hard-cooked egg yolk mixed with softened butter, then shaped.
- Hard-cooked egg white cut in strips, dice or cutouts.
- Raw or cooked green pepper strips or dice.
- Green onion or leek tops, tarragon leaves, nasturtium, violet or geranium leaves, blanched, rinsed in cold water and dried.
- Your choice of the following garnitures.

OTHER GARNITURE IDEAS

• Peel and halve cucumber lengthwise and cut in 3-inch lengths. Place cut side down on board and cut crosswise into slices almost all the way through. Place thinly sliced radish in each cut.
• Spread thinly sliced bread, luncheon meat, cabbage or lettuce leaves with cream cheese, roll and secure with toothpick. Chill and slice 1/2 inch thick.
• Make cream cheese balls with melon baller, roll in finely minced meat, parsley or chives. If desired *just before serving* pierce with small pretzel stick.
• Arrange petals of radish and green pepper on lemon slices.
• Cut small diamonds from cooked or canned beets.
• Cut pickles into shapes with small cutters.
• Deep fry celery leaves, parsley, watercress, chrysanthemum leaves.
• Color cream cheese or mayonnaise with food coloring and use pastry bag to pipe decorations on garnishes or foods.
• Cut aspic into small shapes with cutters and arrange around food to be garnished. Or mound chopped aspic.

OTHER FOODS FOR GARNISHING

Pickled fruits and vegetables of all kinds; parsley, watercress or chervil sprigs; julienne carrots, string beans, or other vegetables; capers; anchovy curls; cherry tomatoes; olives of all kinds, sliced or minced; cheese or bologna cutouts; chutneys (tamarind, gooseberry, mango, peach, cranberry, pineapple); marmalades; broccoli or cauliflower buds; fried onions; prunes; dill weed; kumquats; salted almonds; grated carrots; sieved hard-cooked egg yolk and/or white; flavored butter pipings; chicory, endive or other lettuce; pimientos, shaped or chopped; mint, nasturtium and violet leaves; anchovy paste piping or stars; pomegranate seeds; papaya seeds; truffles, sliced or cut into shapes.

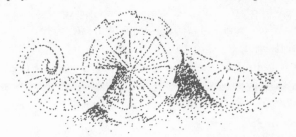

basics: hints

GENERAL COOKING HINTS

• Ovens vary greatly, so watch timing carefully. Never overcrowd oven or cookie sheets.
• Pepper, nutmeg and cheeses should be freshly ground if possible.
• When recipe calls for lemon or lime juice, use freshly squeezed.
• When recipe calls for soy sauce use light soy which is less salty.
• Unless otherwise specified, recipes call for grade A large eggs.
• When sieving hard-cooked eggs use a small sieve with 1/4-inch mesh.
• When baking in glass dishes lower temperature of oven by 25°.
• When possible use Hungarian paprika.
• When recipe calls for seasoned salt, Schilling's is preferred.
• Cucumbers may be scored with a fork or peeled if skin is tough.
• Bruise garlic with flat blade of large knife before peeling.
• To test dishes made of ground fish and meats: Sauté a small amount of mixture and adjust seasonings to taste before proceeding with recipe.

FREEZING

• When freezing phyllo, pasties and the like, place on cookie sheet in freezer. When frozen solid, wrap well. Do not store more than 2 or 3 months.
• The flavor of pepper grows stronger in dishes that are frozen.
• Mayonnaise does not freeze well, although it can be used in a mixture to be frozen a short time.
• *Do not freeze:* hard-cooked egg white, herbs such as parsley and watercress unless minced in a filling, vegetables such as cucumbers, tomatoes and celery unless cooked in a filling or soft cheeses unless in a filling.

STEAMING

To steam without bamboo or other steamer: Place a cake rack or tuna fish can with ends removed in bottom of kettle. Set dish on rack or can; add water to reach no more than 1/2 inch up the side of dish. Bring to boil, wrap lid in tea towel, cover and steam specified time. Caution: while steaming water should remain at a slow boil.

HERB EQUIVALENTS

One-half teaspoon dried herbs or 1/4 teaspoon powdered is equivalent to 1 tablespoon fresh herbs.

breads

spreads/sandwiches/canapes

breads

It may seem sacrilegious that the Earl of Sandwich during England's 1700's covered up the exquisite French "canopy" on a single slice of bread with a second slice, especially to those who revel in the visual artistry of decorated spreads. Yet both open-face canapes and delicate sandwiches make excellent appetizers.

Both require the finest of breads—not too heavy, not too bland; not crumbly, rubbery or diaphanous—along with imaginative spreads and fillers to make them fit for entertaining. European breads often outshine American commercial products in flavor and consistency, though the latter, because they're soft and resilient, are well suited for rolled or pinwheel sandwiches. Fine specialty breads can be found, especially at local bakeries, or baked at home with less effort than you might think.

Spreads, including butter, should be evenly distributed over entire surface. Both spreads and fillings should complement, not mask the flavor of the bread—e.g. ham on rye or watercress on white. Color combinations play an important role.

It is easier to slice frozen or partially frozen bread, while spreads and fillings should be applied at room temperature. Butter and cream cheese help "seal" against watery ingredients that would otherwise make the bread soggy. Even then, tomatoes, cucumbers, asparagus, etc., present problems if added too far ahead.

The consistency of the spread or filling used depends upon what it is being used for. For rolls, the filling should be firm. For stuffing tomatoes, beets or artichoke hearts or for spreading on bread or crackers a medium consistency is best.

BROWN BREAD

3 tablespoons butter
1/2 cup white or brown sugar
1 egg, beaten
1-1/2 tablespoons freshly grated orange peel (optional)
1 cup unbleached white flour
1 teaspoon each salt and baking soda
1/2 teaspoon each cinnamon, nutmeg and powdered ginger
1/4 teaspoon ground cloves
1 cup whole-wheat flour
1/2 cup molasses
1 cup buttermilk
2/3 cup raisins

Cream butter and sugar; add egg and orange peel and beat well. Sift white flour with salt, baking soda and spices. Add alternately with whole-wheat flour and molasses and buttermilk. Blend well and stir in raisins. Pour into a buttered loaf pan or into 3 6x3-1/2-inch loaf pans. Bake in 350° oven 50 minutes (35 minutes for small loaves) or until toothpick inserted in center comes out clean and bread has shrunk slightly from sides of pan. Cool 10 minutes and turn out onto rack. Serve thinly sliced either warm or cool with sweet butter and/or cream cheese.
Makes 1 large loaf or 3 small

POTATO BREAD

3 medium potatoes
water to cover
2 tablespoons dry yeast
1/2 cup warm evaporated milk
2 tablespoons each butter or lard and sugar
2 teaspoons salt
about 5-1/2 cups unbleached flour
salad oil for greasing

Bring potatoes and water to boil, cover and cook over medium heat until potatoes are soft. Drain and reserve water. Peel potatoes and mash while still hot. Reserve. Dissolve yeast in 1/2 cup of the warm potato water. Combine with another cup of potato water, milk, 2 cups mashed potatoes, butter or lard, sugar and salt. Add flour and blend well. Turn out on floured board and knead 10 minutes or more until elastic and smooth, adding more flour if needed to prevent sticking. Place in greased bowl and grease top lightly. Cover with tea towel and let rise in warm place until double in bulk, about 1-1/2 hours. Punch down, knead briefly and divide in thirds. Place in 3 greased bread pans, cover with tea towel and let rise in warm place until double. Bake in 375° oven 40 minutes until golden and bread shrinks away from sides of pan. Cool on rack 10 minutes and turn out onto rack.
Makes 3 loaves

EGG BREAD

2 tablespoons dry yeast
2 cups warm water
1 tablespoon salt
1/2 cup sugar
3/4 cup vegetable oil
4 eggs, beaten
1/2 cup soy flour
about 7 cups unbleached flour
salad oil for greasing
beaten egg yolks

Sprinkle yeast over warm water and let stand 5 minutes. Stir to dissolve. Add salt, sugar, oil, eggs, soy flour and about half of the unbleached flour. Stir well and add remaining flour. Turn out onto floured board, adding flour if needed to prevent sticking and knead at least 10 minutes or until dough is smooth and elastic. Place in oiled bowl and turn dough to coat all sides. Cover with tea towel and let rise in warm place 1-1/2 hours or until double in size. Punch down, knead briefly and form into 3 loaves. Place in 3 greased loaf pans and cover with tea towel. Let rise in warm place 1 hour or until double in size. Brush with beaten egg yolk and bake in 350° oven 45 minutes or until golden and bread pulls away from sides of pan.
Makes 3 loaves

breads

CHIVE BREAD

1 tablespoon dry yeast
1/4 cup warm water
1 cup creamed cottage cheese
1/4 teaspoon baking soda
1 tablespoon melted butter
1 egg, beaten
1 teaspoon salt
1/4 cup minced chives
2-1/4 cups flour
salad oil for greasing

In large bowl dissolve yeast in water. Mix in cheese, baking soda, butter, egg, salt and chives. Beat in flour and turn out on floured board. Knead, adding flour as needed, until smooth and no longer sticky. Place in greased bowl, spread top with oil, cover with tea towel and let rise in warm place 1-1/2 hours or until double. Punch down and transfer to greased loaf pan. Cover with tea towel and let rise in warm place 1 hour or until double in bulk. Bake in 350° oven 40 to 50 minutes, remove from oven, turn out on rack and cool.
Makes 1 loaf

WHOLE WHEAT/RYE BREAD

2 tablespoons dry yeast
1/2 cup lukewarm water
1-1/2 cups milk, scalded
4 tablespoons butter
1/2 cup honey
1 tablespoon salt
3 cups unbleached white flour
3 cups wheat or rye flour
salad oil for greasing

Sprinkle yeast over warm water and let stand 5 minutes. Stir to dissolve. Combine milk, butter, honey and salt; cool to lukewarm. Add yeast. Beat in flours and turn out on floured board. Knead, adding extra flour if needed to keep from sticking, at least 10 minutes or until dough is smooth and elastic. Place in lightly oiled bowl and turn dough to coat with oil. Cover with tea towel and let rise in warm place 1-1/2 hours or until double in size. Punch down, divide evenly and place each half in greased bread pan. Cover with tea towel and let rise in warm place 1 hour or until double in size. Bake in 375° oven 30 minutes or until golden and bread pulls away from sides of pans. Remove to rack for 10 minutes and turn out onto rack to cool.
Makes 2 loaves

PUMPKIN BREAD

5 cups all-purpose flour
4 cups sugar
4 teaspoons baking soda
1 teaspoon salt
2 teaspoons cinnamon
1 teaspoon ground cloves
1 cup vegetable oil
1 #2-1/2 can pumpkin

Combine dry ingredients in large bowl. With a spoon make a well and add salad oil and pumpkin. Mix with a large wooden paddle or sturdy wooden spoon until well blended. Pour into 2 greased loaf pans and bake in a 350° oven for about 1 hour and 15 minutes, or until a toothpick inserted comes out dry. To freeze, wrap securely in foil.
Makes 2 loaves

CORNUCOPIAS

Trim crusts of thin-sliced bread, cut into 2-1/2-inch squares and brush with melted butter or seasoned butter. Twist to make cornucopia shape, fastening the overlapping opposite corners with a toothpick. Place on buttered cookie sheet and toast in 350° oven until golden. Remove toothpick, cool and store in airtight container. When ready to use, fill with cold choux fillings or spreads and fillings of choice.

CROÛTES

Slice stale bread 1 inch thick, cut 2-inch rounds and with smaller cutter press down on round halfway through. Deep fry, drain on paper toweling and remove center. Fill with choux filling or spreads and fillings of choice.

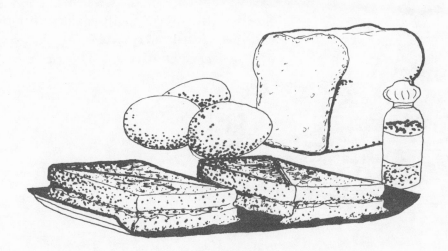

breads

MELBA TOASTS

From thinly sliced white bread or cocktail rye cut 1-1/2- to 2-inch rounds or cutouts with canape cutters. Brush with melted butter or seasoned butter and place on oiled baking sheet. Bake in a 400° oven until golden and crisp. Or, broil to brown on one side, brush other side with melted butter or seasoned butter and bake buttered side up in a 300° oven 30 minutes or until crisp. Cool and store in airtight container 3 to 4 days. Or freeze up to 2 months.

Buttered side can also be sprinkled with a choice of herbs such as marjoram, thyme, savory, oregano, paprika, etc. before crisping.

Packaged melba rounds are available but they are expensive and many rounds are broken in shipping.

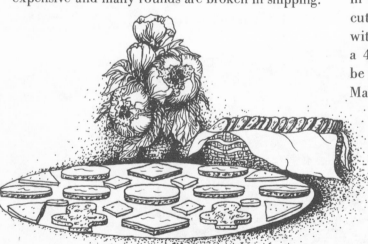

CHEESE CUTOUTS

1 cup flour
1/2 teaspoon beau monde seasoning
1/4 teaspoon onion powder
1/8 teaspoon cayenne pepper
1 tablespoon dried herbs (optional)
1/3 cup butter
1/2 cup grated sharp Cheddar, Monterey Jack, Emmenthaler or Gruyère cheese
2 to 3 teaspoons dry white wine
1 egg, slightly beaten
dill, caraway, sesame or celery seeds

Sift flour, seasoning, onion powder and cayenne. Add herbs and cut in butter. Blend in cheese and just enough wine to moisten. Form into ball, wrap in wax paper and chill 1 hour. Roll 1/8 inch thick, cut into desired shapes, brush with egg and sprinkle with dill, caraway, sesame or celery seeds. Bake in a 450° oven 8 to 10 minutes or until golden. May be frozen and reheated.

Makes approximately 3 dozen

SEASONED BUTTERS

For each 1/4 pound softened butter cream in:
- *Mustard:* 2 to 3 tablespoons homemade mustard or prepared mustard.
- *Watercress:* 1/2 cup finely chopped watercress, 1 tablespoon lemon juice, 1/4 teaspoon marjoram, 1/8 teaspoon onion powder. (Optional: anchovy paste to taste.)
- *Almond:* 1/2 cup finely ground almonds.
- *Salmon or lox:* 1-1/2 ounces mashed salmon or lox.
- *Sardine or anchovy:* 1 tablespoon sardine or anchovy paste, 1 teaspoon lemon juice (best with sweet butter).
- *Garlic:* 1/2 to 1 teaspoon pressed garlic, 2 tablespoons each grated Parmesan cheese and minced parsley, 1 teaspoon paprika.
- *Mushroom:* Sauté 1 cup minced mushrooms in 2 tablespoons butter with 1 tablespoon lemon juice 10 minutes. Mash to a paste and season to taste with salt, oregano or savory, paprika, chives, white pepper and cayenne pepper.
- *Paprika-onion:* Sauté 1/2 cup minced onion in 2 tablespoons butter until soft. Add 2 to 3 teaspoons paprika.
- *Onion:* 2 tablespoons finely minced onions and 1/2 teaspoon Worcestershire sauce.
- *Cheese:* 4 ounces blue cheese, crumbled, 1 teaspoon each lemon juice and minced chives.
- *Horseradish:* 1 to 2 teaspoons prepared horseradish.
- *Chive/green onion:* 1/3 cup finely minced chives or green onions and 1 teaspoon lemon juice.
- *Lemon:* 2 tablespoons each lemon juice and finely minced parsley and 1 teaspoon grated lemon rind.
- *Herb:* 1 tablespoon each minced parsley, chervil and chives and 1 teaspoon finely minced basil or tarragon.
- *Parsley or chervil:* 1/3 cup minced parsley or 1/4 cup minced chervil and 1/2 teaspoon or more grated lemon rind.
- *Dill:* 2 tablespoons minced fresh dill weed, 1 teaspoon lemon juice and 1 to 2 drops Tabasco.
- *Egg yolk:* 3 hard-cooked egg yolks, mashed, and 1/2 teaspoon paprika.
- *Tarragon:* 2 tablespoons minced tarragon and 2 teaspoons lemon juice.
- *Shrimp:* 1/2 pound cooked shrimp *finely* minced or ground, 1 tablespoon lime or lemon juice, 1/2 teaspoon fish seasoning (optional).
- *Curry:* 2 tablespoons minced shallots sautéed in 2 teaspoons butter and curry powder to taste.
- *Tomato:* 1/2 cup peeled, seeded and finely chopped and drained tomatoes forced through sieve and 1 teaspoon lemon juice.
- *Mixed:* 1 tablespoon each finely minced capers, chives, sweet gherkins, anchovy and pickled onion and 1 teaspoon minced tarragon.
- *Chutney:* 2 tablespoons finely minced chutney and curry powder to taste.
- *Rosemary:* 1 to 2 teaspoons fresh rosemary.
- *Maple:* 1/4 cup maple syrup.

spreads

EGGPLANT SPREAD

1 large (1-1/2 pounds) eggplant
2 cloves garlic, minced
1/4 cup olive oil
1/4 cup salad oil
2 large tomatoes, peeled and chopped
    (about 1-1/2 cups)
1 large onion, chopped
2 tablespoons lemon juice
1 teaspoon salt
1/8 teaspoon cayenne pepper
2 tablespoons minced parsley

Bake eggplant in 400° oven 1/2 hour, or until soft to the touch. Peel and chop. In a large skillet, sauté garlic lightly in olive and salad oil. Add eggplant, tomatoes, onion, lemon juice, salt and cayenne. Cook over low heat, stirring frequently, until mixture is thickened to a spreading consistency. Chill. To serve, place mixture in the center of a platter and sprinkle liberally with minced parsley. Surround with crackers or thinly sliced dark bread, buttered.
Makes about 3 cups

AVOCADO BUTTER

2 avocados
1/4 cup lemon or lime juice
1/3 cup butter, softened
1 envelope gelatin
1/2 cup half-and-half
1/2 teaspoon each salt, garlic powder,
    paprika and white pepper

Mash avocados with lemon or lime juice and cream thoroughly into butter. Soften gelatin in half-and-half and dissolve over hot water. Add to avocado-butter mixture and season. Adjust to taste and pack into 2-cup crock. Chill.
Makes approximately 1-1/2 cups

SALMON SPREAD

1 7-3/4-ounce can salmon, drained and flaked
1/4 cup mayonnaise
dash salt
black pepper to taste
1 tablespoon finely chopped green onions
1 teaspoon lemon juice
capers

Combine salmon, mayonnaise, salt, pepper, onions and lemon juice in an attractive bowl and garnish with capers. Serve with crisp crackers or thin slices of buttered pumpernickel bread.
Makes approximately 1-1/2 cups

PORT-CHEDDAR SPREAD

1 13-1/4-ounce can crushed pineapple
8 ounces cream cheese, softened
2 cups shredded Cheddar cheese
1/3 cup port wine
1 tablespoon seasoned salt
1 teaspoon garlic powder
1/4 teaspoon dry mustard
2 tablespoons minced parsley

Drain pineapple well. Beat softened cream cheese with Cheddar cheese and wine until smooth. Beat in seasoned salt, garlic powder and mustard. Fold in parsley and drained pineapple. Spoon into crocks and chill well before serving. Stores well.
Makes approximately 3 cups

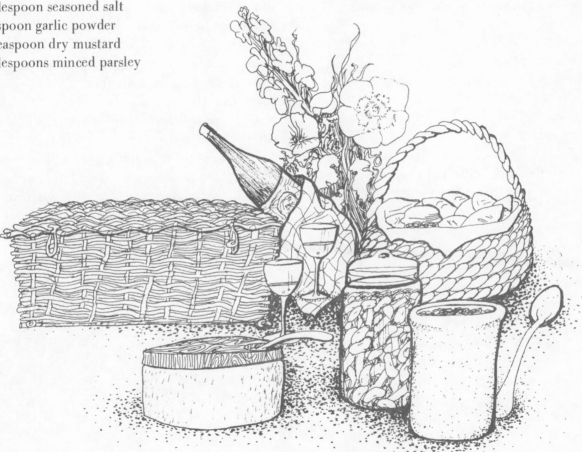

spreads

COTTAGE CHEESE SPREAD

1-1/2 cups creamed small curd cottage cheese
1/4 pound Gorgonzola cheese, crumbled
1/3 cup softened butter
2 tablespoons minced chives
2 teaspoons each anchovy paste and paprika
1/4 cup beer

Presentation
1/4 cup each finely minced green pepper,
   radishes and parsley
caraway seeds
melba rounds or crackers

Combine ingredients and adjust seasonings to taste, adding more beer if needed for spreading consistency. Chill.
Mound spread on serving platter and garnish with pepper, radishes and parsley. Place a bowl of caraway seeds in one corner of platter and arrange melba rounds or crackers around spread.
Makes approximately 50 buffet servings

LEMON CURD

2 whole eggs
2 egg yolks
1-1/4 cups sugar
1 teaspoon grated lemon rind (more if desired)
2/3 cup lemon juice
1/2 pound butter, melted

Combine whole eggs, egg yolks and sugar. Beat with electric mixer until thick, 3 to 5 minutes. Carefully stir in lemon rind, lemon juice and melted butter. Beat 2 minutes or until blended thoroughly.
Pour mixture into the top of a double boiler. Cook, stirring constantly, over hot, not boiling, water until mixture thickens. Remove from heat and cool completely. Spoon into small crocks or pretty jars and cover tightly. Store in refrigerator. Serve with water biscuits or crackers.
Makes about 3 cups

POTTED SHRIMP

1/4 pound butter
1/4 teaspoon each mace and nutmeg, or
   1/2 teaspoon curry powder
1/16 teaspoon cayenne pepper
1 pound small cooked shrimp
2 teaspoons lemon juice
1 teaspoon onion juice (optional)
clarified butter*

*See glossary

Melt butter; add mace and nutmeg or curry powder and cayenne pepper. Add shrimp, lemon juice and onion juice and stir to coat shrimp. Carefully pack, so as not to mash shrimp, into 2 10-ounce crocks. Allow to cool. When cool, pour enough melted clarified butter over top of shrimp mixture to completely cover. Keep refrigerated. Serve as a spread for crackers or thin slices of brown bread. Makes approximately 2 cups

SWISS CHEESE SPREAD

1/3 cup mayonnaise
1 tablespoon dry vermouth
1/2 teaspoon lemon juice
1/4 teaspoon prepared mustard
dash each of salt, white pepper, garlic
   powder and nutmeg
2 cups finely grated Swiss or Monterey
   Jack cheese

Thoroughly combine the mayonnaise, vermouth, lemon juice, mustard and seasonings. Add cheese and mix well. Spoon into attractive pottery crock, cover and chill. Or form into roll, wrap in wax paper, chill, roll in toasted sesame seeds and serve surrounded by assorted crackers.
Makes approximately 1-1/2 cups

spreads

SPREADS AND FILLINGS

Mix together any of the following combinations.
- 4 ounces softened cream cheese, 1/2 cup each minced watercress and finely chopped walnuts, 2 sieved hard-cooked eggs, salt, white pepper and paprika to taste, cream or French dressing to make spreading consistency.
- Equal amounts softened cream cheese and minced cucumber; season with grated onion, salt and white pepper to taste; add mayonnaise to make spreading consistency.
- 1/2 cup each mayonnaise and cooked crumbled bacon; season with minced dill pickles and pepper to taste.
- Softened cream cheese, sieved pimientos, salt and white pepper to taste, mayonnaise to make spreading consistency.
- Avocado, lime or lemon juice, salt and white pepper to taste.
- Softened cream cheese and currant jelly.
- 1 cup finely minced celery, 1 tablespoon finely chopped walnuts, mayonnaise to spreading consistency, cayenne pepper to taste.
- Ground cooked chicken, finely minced water chestnuts, mayonnaise to make spreading consistency, salt and pepper to taste.
- 3 ounces cream cheese, mayonnaise to spreading consistency, 1/4 cup chopped black olives, 2 tablespoons finely minced green pepper, onion juice, salt, white pepper and bits of pimiento to taste.
- 3 ounces cream cheese, mayonnaise to spreading consistency, 1 3-1/2-ounce package dried beef, finely minced, 2 sieved hard-cooked eggs, 1/3 cup finely grated sharp Cheddar cheese, salt and pepper to taste.
- 1/2 cup small curd cottage cheese, 2 tablespoons crumbled blue cheese and finely chopped radishes (or use radish cutouts as garnish).
- Softened cream cheese, white Dubonnet, anchovy paste, minced chives and Worcestershire sauce to taste (garnish with ripe olive halves).
- 1 4-3/8-ounce can sardines, drained and mashed, 2 tablespoons minced parsley, 2 teaspoons minced shallots, 1 tablespoon lemon juice, salt and pepper to taste (garnish with parsley sprig).
- 4 ounces cream cheese, 2 tablespoons minced parsley, 1/2 teaspoon pressed garlic, 1/2 cup finely chopped, peeled, seeded tomato, salt and white pepper to taste.
- 1/2 cup mayonnaise, 2 sieved hard-cooked eggs, 1/2 cup each minced radishes, watercress and cucumber (salt, let stand, drain and dry before mincing), 1/4 cup minced green onion, 1 tablespoon fresh minced dill weed, salt, white pepper and mustard to taste.
- 1/2 cup mayonnaise, 1 cup minced cooked or canned shrimp, 1 tablespoon minced shallots or 2 tablespoons minced green onion and tops, 1 to 2 teaspoons drained capers and white pepper to taste.
- 3 ounces cream cheese, 1 2-1/4-ounce can deviled ham, grated onion, prepared horseradish, salt and pepper to taste.
- 1/2 cup shredded cooked lobster, 1 sieved hard-cooked egg, 2 tablespoons minced cucumber (salt,

let stand, drain and dry before mincing), mayonnaise to spreading consistency, salt and pepper to taste.

• 4 hard-cooked eggs, finely chopped, 2 slices cooked and crumbled bacon, mayonnaise to spreading consistency, Worcestershire sauce, salt and pepper to taste.

• 3 ounces cream cheese, 1 tablespoon grated orange rind, 1 to 2 tablespoons finely chopped pecans, mayonnaise to spreading consistency, salt and paprika to taste.

• 4 ounces cream cheese, 1/2 cup finely minced raw mushrooms, 1 teaspoon lemon juice, onion juice, garlic powder, salt and pepper to taste; add cream if thinning is needed.

• 3 ounces cream cheese, 1/4 cup sour cream, onion powder, garlic powder, Worcestershire sauce and anchovy paste to taste.

• 1/2 cup each finely minced ham and chicken, 2 tablespoons each finely chopped Brazil nuts and chives, 1 tablespoon finely minced gherkin, mayonnaise to spreading consistency, salt and pepper to taste.

• Ground ham, minced pickle, mayonnaise to spreading consistency, allspice and pepper to taste.

• 1/2 cup each minced cooked tongue and chicken or turkey, 4 tablespoons softened butter, Dijon-style mustard, salt and pepper to taste.

• 1 cup minced watercress, 4 ounces softened cream cheese, 1/2 teaspoon each salt and paprika, 1/4 teaspoon curry powder, mayonnaise to spreading consistency.

• 1/2 cup each mayonnaise and minced celery, 1 tablespoon minced onion, 1/2 teaspoon each salt and curry powder, 1/4 teaspoon each dry mustard and Tabasco; add 4 hard-cooked eggs, finely chopped and adjust to taste.

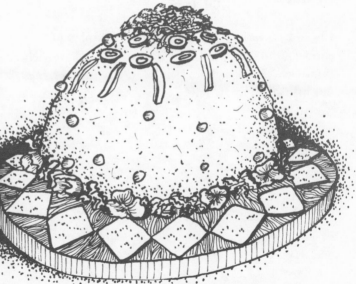

sandwiches

PINWHEEL SANDWICHES

Slice Pullman (sandwich-type) bread lengthwise into 1/4-inch slices. Remove crusts, spread with seasoned butter and spread or filling and cut in half crosswise. Place on slightly dampened tea towel. From long end roll each half like a jelly roll and seal seam with a little butter. Wrap in wax paper, being sure seam is secure. Wrap in heavy foil if freezing or in slightly dampened tea towel if refrigerating.

Cut in 1/4-inch slices and arrange on serving platter. Garnish and cover with saran wrap. Refrigerate until ready to serve.

STACKED SANDWICHES

Choose a variety of breads' and complementary spreads and fillings. Use 4 slices of bread to each sandwich. Wrap well and chill. Just before serving, cut into small sandwiches.

ROLLED SANDWICHES

Remove crusts from thinly sliced bread and flatten slices with rolling pin. Spread with butter and/or cream cheese and filling of choice. Place slices on slightly dampened tea towel, roll tightly like a jelly roll and seal seam with butter. Wrap in wax paper, being sure seam is secure. Wrap in heavy foil if freezing or in slightly dampened tea towel if refrigerating.

To serve hot
Cut matching diagonals off each end of roll and place on buttered cookie sheets. Spread a little butter on top and bake in 350° oven 10 minutes or until golden.

Extra suggestions
• Drain and dry asparagus spears and place on bread; roll as directed.
• Salt, drain and dry fingers of cucumber; place on bread and roll as directed.
• Place watercress sprigs on bread and roll as directed.

Filling suggestions
• Softened butter seasoned with curry powder, pressed garlic, minced herbs and grated Parmesan cheese
• Mushroom or tomato-ham duxelle (page 12)
• Chicken spread

PETA SANDWICHES

Slit pockets in Mideast peta bread (see glossary) and set aside. Just before serving, heat in 350° oven 30 seconds. Guests fill bread pocket with filling and/or condiment selections and eat like a sandwich. The following filling recipes serve 8 to 10. Serve with tabooleh salad.

• *Filling I* Combine 2 pounds ground lean beef, 2 tablespoons minced mint, 2 teaspoons finely minced garlic, 1-1/2 teaspoons salt and 1/2 teaspoon pepper. Chill and form into 1-inch balls. Brown in heavy skillet, drain off fat and add 3 cups buttermilk. Bring to gentle boil and simmer 10 minutes or until meat is just done. Serve with yoghurt sauce.

• *Filling II* Marinate 2 pounds lean lamb (leg) cut into 1/2-inch cubes with mint marinade, double recipe (page 143). Barbecue meat as directed. Serve with selected condiments.

• *Condiments:* garbanzo beans and minced onion marinated in vinegar, oil and pepper; cut-up artichoke hearts; halved black olives; seeded and minced canned hot green peppers; peeled, seeded and minced tomato, minced cucumber, green pepper, zucchini and parsley in any combination; yoghurt sauce; stringy Monterey Jack cheese, shredded.

• *Filling III* Combine 2 cups shredded lettuce, 2 hard-cooked eggs, chopped, 1 diced avocado tossed in 1 tablespoon lemon juice and 1 tablespoon crumbled blue cheese. Bind with French dressing.

• *Filling IV* Sauté 1-1/2 pounds lean ground beef with 1/2 cup minced onion, 1 teaspoon salt, 1/2 teaspoon pepper and 1/4 teaspoon garlic powder. Mash 1 15-ounce can red kidney beans and add to meat. Season to taste with Tabasco and simmer until thick. Serve with lettuce and tomato slices.

sandwiches

TABOOLEH

1 cup fine-grain bulghur
warm water
1 large head romaine lettuce
2 finely chopped, medium-sized tomatoes
1-1/2 cups chopped green onions with tops
1 cup minced parsley
3/4 cup minced mint

Dressing
1/3 cup olive oil
1/4 cup lemon juice
1 teaspoon salt
1-1/2 teaspoons allspice

Place bulghur in a large bowl with enough warm water to cover. Set aside for 3/4 to 1 hour. Drain and squeeze grain to extract as much moisture as possible. Separate leaves of romaine, wash, blot dry and chill until ready to serve.

Combine dressing ingredients and mix well. Combine bulghur, tomato, onions, parsley and mint. Shake dressing and pour over bulghur mixture. Toss until all dressing is absorbed. Line a large platter with the chilled romaine leaves. Arrange bulghur mixture in the center of the platter. Traditionally, a guest is to use a broken section of the romaine to scoop up a portion of bulghur. The romaine is then pinched together to secure the grain as it is eaten.

COLD CANAPES

Use a variety of shapes of *fresh* bread cutouts—rounds, ovals, fingers, rectangles, diamonds, etc. Or use crackers or fried bread for a base. For fried bread, the bread may be several days old and is fried on both sides in butter or deep oil.

For the suggestions that follow, any bread shape is appropriate unless otherwise specified. The ingredients are mentioned in the order they are to be layered. Pipe decorations on with a pastry tube. When using meats, cheeses, smoked fish, etc., they should be very thinly sliced; place them on bread before cutting into desired shapes for a perfectly formed canape. Then decorate. Save any bread crusts and scraps for making bread crumbs, puddings, etc.

• Sweet butter, rolled caper-filled anchovy with a little of its oil.

• Sweet butter, cooked shrimp halved lengthwise, sprinkling of paprika, garnish of parsley.

• Sweet butter, mustard, slice of Gruyère cheese, rows of thinly sliced radishes.

• Horseradish butter, tiny roll of thinly sliced rare roast beef, garnish of chopped green onion.

• Butter, slice of tomato, sprinkling of sieved hard-cooked eggs, anchovy curl in center.

• Sweet butter, spread of equal parts crumbled Gorgonzola cheese, cream cheese and crushed pineapple, garnish of seedless grapes halved lengthwise.

• Almond butter, thin slice of chicken or turkey, garnish of watercress.

• Avocado butter, shrimp or crab, garnish of tiny lemon peel.

• Shrimp butter, flaked crab, border of piped shrimp butter, drained caper and parsley leaf in center.

• Horseradish butter, Esrom or other creamy semi-soft cheese, slice of cherry tomato, overlapping tiny shrimp, sprinkling of finely minced parsley.

• Butter, swirls of cream cheese colored with food coloring and flavored with anchovy paste.

• Bread diamond, salmon butter, cooked or canned (drain and pat dry) asparagus spear set on diagonal, garnish of canned pimiento strips.

• Bread diamond, butter, slice of cherry tomato spread with mixture of lumpfish caviar, hard-cooked egg yolk and lemon juice, garnish of tiny lemon peel twist on either end.

• Bread rectangle, 3 narrow strips Gruyère cheese, row of tiny shrimp in between, dots of mayonnaise, garnish of tiny parsley sprig.

• Bread rectangle, sweet butter, deviled ham, cross bars of cheese strips, garnish of tiny green pepper and canned pimiento strips.

• Bread rectangle, butter, slice of tomato, slice of hard-cooked egg, anchovy curl on each end, sprinkling of chopped chives.

• Bread round, butter, slice of tiny canned beet, slice of cucumber or onion, garnish of hard-cooked egg white.

• Rye bread, steak tartare, border of tiny shrimp, dab of raw egg yolk center.

• Dark rye, butter, sour cream mixed with horseradish and Worcestershire sauce, slice of corned

cold canapes

beef, blanched shredded cabbage tossed with vinegar, caraway seeds and salt and pepper to taste.
• Dark rye or pumpernickel, mock liver pâté, slice of sweet red onion, dab of sour cream and caviar, garnish of tiny lemon peel.
• Bread, butter, mustard mayonnaise, shredded lettuce, ham roll-up.
• Rye bread, steak tartare, border of onion, well of caviar, decoration of grated horseradish, capers and sieved hard-cooked eggs.
• Rye bread round, butter, mustard, thinly sliced ham round, slice of hearts of palm, tiny piece of canned pimiento.
• Rye bread, mustard butter, thinly sliced tongue, sliced pimiento-stuffed olive, parsley sprig center, sieved hard-cooked egg border.
• Rye rectangle, butter, cornucopias of ham slices filled with chicken liver pâté, set diagonally, garnish of tiny pickle.
• Pumpernickel rounds, anchovy butter, marinated artichoke bottom drained and filled with piping of cream cheese softened with sour cream, garnish of watercress.
• Rye bread, sweet butter mashed with lox, anchovy paste, lemon juice, dill weed and pepper, topping of caper.
• Dark rye bread stars, pitted ripe olive filled with cream cheese seasoned with prepared horseradish, garnish of cream cheese on each star point.
• Fried bread, spread of anchovy butter, sieved hard-cooked egg yolk and few drops of olive oil, sprinkling of sieved hard-cooked egg white.

• Toast, spread of equal parts grated cheese and butter, decoration of thin slices of gherkin and canned pimiento.
• Toast, spread of canned pâté de foie gras and butter, decoration of canned pimiento and hard-cooked egg cutouts.
• Melba or fried bread rounds, slice of hard-cooked egg, border of watercress butter piping, watercress sprig in center.
• Fried bread or melba round, thin slice of onion, slice of marinated and drained cucumber, dab of lumpfish caviar, lemon juice, minced chives, border of sieved hard-cooked egg.
• Bread diamonds, seasoned butter, roll-ups placed lengthwise on diamond, decoration of garnishes that complement the roll-ups.
• Bread, ham, coating of aspic made with minced parsley.
• Butter, spread of equal parts cream cheese and mayonnaise, slice of inside strip of peeled tomato, dab of cream cheese, garnish of chopped chives or tiny piece of lox.
• Tomato butter, slice of lobster, black olive half, light coating of fish aspic, border of hard-cooked egg mixed with mayonnaise.
• Butter, salmon salad, decoration of sliced and slivered black olive.
• Butter, sardine spread, hard-cooked egg-white petals, black olive half center, sprinkling of sieved hard-cooked egg yolk.
• Butter, cream cheese, sprinkling of dill weed, tiny lemon peel.

- Butter, piped cream cheese, daisy design of slivered blanched almonds, hard-cooked egg yolk center.
- Bread round, butter, thinly sliced red onion rounds to fit bread, sprinkling of Mexican-Style Hot Lemon Seasoning*, dab of mayonnaise, garnish of caper and chopped chives or parsley.
- Bread round, watercress butter, slice of mushroom rubbed with lemon juice, piece of canned pimiento on either side of mushroom stem.
- Bread diamond, spread of minced sautéed mushrooms, minced ham, cream cheese, salt and pepper, garnish of parsley.
- Butter, sliced cucumbers (sprinkle with salt, let stand, drain and pat dry), sprinkling of white pepper or paprika.

- Cream cheese, thinly sliced lox; sprinkle with dill weed.
- Butter, slice of mock liver pâté, thin slice of tomato, thin slice of onion.
- Stoned wheat thins, butter, thin slice of sharp Cheddar cheese, generous sprinkling of celery salt to taste.
- Rye or whole-wheat bread, mixture of butter, chopped black olives and liverwurst; garnish of halved black olive.
- Bread or crackers, cream cheese seasoned with anchovy fillets mashed with their oil, prepared mustard and additional oil to taste; garnish of tiny parsley sprig.

*See glossary

cold canapes

ASPIC CANAPES

1 envelope gelatin
3 tablespoons dry sherry
1 cup mayonnaise
1-1/2 tablespoons lemon juice
3 tablespoons minced parsley
1 tablespoon each minced chives and green pepper
1/2 teaspoon salt
1/4 teaspoon white pepper
1/2 cup heavy cream, whipped
1/2 cup flaked crab meat or diced cooked shrimp
buttered 2-1/4-inch bread rounds
tiny parsley sprigs
hard-cooked egg white bits or
　　small strips of pimiento

Soften gelatin in sherry and dissolve over hot water. Combine with mayonnaise, lemon juice, parsley, chives, green pepper, salt and pepper. Fold in cream and chill until partially set. Fold in crab or shrimp and pour into 3 6-ounce orange juice cans that have been rinsed in cold water. Chill at least 6 hours. Open other end of can and push aspic out. Cut into 1/4-inch slices. Place slices on bread rounds and garnish with parsley and egg or pimiento.
Makes approximately 3 dozen

CHICKEN ROLL CANAPES

3 large chicken breasts, boned, skinned and halved
2 tablespoons each soy sauce and oil
1/4 cup sake or dry sherry
1 garlic clove, pressed or finely minced
1 teaspoon finely minced ginger root
3 tablespoons butter, melted
rye or white bread rounds slightly larger than
　　the chicken slices
butter
mustard or herb mayonnaise
pimiento bits
parsley sprigs
vegetable jelly (page 17)

Being careful not to tear, pound chicken breasts between wax paper to flatten. Combine soy sauce, oil, sake, garlic and ginger root. Marinate chicken in soy mixture at least 4 hours. Starting at long side, roll each breast tightly like a jelly roll and tie with string to hold in place. Place in shallow baking dish and pour marinade and butter over. Bake in 325° oven 1/2 hour, basting and turning often. Cool, refrigerate and slice thinly. Spread bread rounds with butter and mustard or mayonnaise. Top with chicken slice and garnish with pimiento and tiny bit of parsley. Coat with jelly, chill to set aspic, cover with saran wrap and refrigerate no longer than 3 hours.
Makes approximately 5 dozen

HOT CANAPE SUGGESTIONS

Toast bread rounds on one side, flip over and cool. Spread untoasted side with any of the following. Broil before serving.

• Butter, thin slice of red onion, grated or shredded cheese, sprinkling of paprika.

• Butter, slice of water chestnut, slice of Cheddar or Monterey Jack cheese, sprinkling of minced parsley on one half, paprika on the other.

• Butter, grated Cheddar cheese combined with minced ham, chopped olives and minced chutney, sprinkling of grated Parmesan cheese.

• Mixture of 4 ounces cream cheese, 1 7-1/2-ounce can minced clams (drained), 1 teaspoon grated onion, 2 tablespoons minced chives; season to taste with garlic powder, white pepper and Worcestershire sauce; sprinkle with paprika.

• Mixture of 2 tablespoons soft butter, 1/4 cup finely minced cooked shrimp, 2 teaspoons minced chives, 1 teaspoon soy sauce, 2 tablespoons finely minced water chestnuts, 2 to 3 tablespoons sour cream to make firm spreading consistency; after broiling top with tiny cooked shrimp and parsley.

• Mixture of 1 cup flaked crab meat, 1/4 cup grated Gruyère cheese, 1 tablespoon dry white wine, mayonnaise to make firm spreading consistency, sprinkling of paprika.

• Mixture of avocado mashed with lemon juice, salt, garlic powder and Tabasco to taste, tiny bit of bacon, sprinkling of paprika.

• Pumpernickel, butter, Münster, Cheddar or Monterey Jack cheese, thinly sliced onion.

• French bread roll slices, mixture of equal amounts grated Romano or Parmesan cheese and mayonnaise, sherry or Marsala to taste.

• Rye, mixture of 1 4-1/2-ounce can chopped olives, 1/4 cup minced green onion and tops, 1/4 teaspoon finely minced garlic, 3/4 cup grated sharp Cheddar cheese, mayonnaise to make firm spreading consistency, curry powder to taste. After broiling garnish with tiny parsley sprig.

• Butter, thin slice of sharp Cheddar cheese, dab of mango or other chutney.

• Mixture of 4 ounces softened cream cheese, 2 tablespoons sour cream, 1-1/2 cups finely minced raw mushrooms, 1 tablespoon finely minced onion, 1/4 teaspoon each salt and garlic powder, minced tarragon and lemon juice to taste, sprinkling of paprika.

• Mixture of 1/4 pound butter, 1/2 teaspoon pressed garlic and 1 to 2 tablespoons seeded and finely minced canned hot green chilies (may be frozen at this point), topping of finely grated Cheddar or Monterey Jack cheese mixed with equal amount of mayonnaise.

• Mixture of 4 tablespoons soft butter, 1/4 cup finely minced raw mushrooms, 2 tablespoons grated Gruyère cheese, 1 tablespoon finely minced shallots, salt and white pepper to taste, sprinkling of paprika.

• Mixture of 1 cup flaked crab meat, 1/4 cup grated Gruyère cheese, 1 tablespoon dry white wine, mayonnaise to make firm spreading consistency, sprinkling of paprika.

• Mustard, thin slice of ham or chilled canned corned beef, sprinkling of grated Gruyère cheese.

hot canapes

MUSHROOM CANAPES

8 ounces cream cheese, softened
1/2 pound mushrooms, very finely minced
1 tablespoon grated onion
3 tablespoons minced chives
1-1/2 teaspoons lemon juice
1/2 teaspoon each Worcestershire sauce and salt
1/4 teaspoon each white pepper and garlic powder
2 to 3 drops Tabasco
6 to 7 dozen bread cutouts
paprika

Combine cheese, mushrooms, onion, chives, lemon juice and seasonings. Adjust seasonings and chill. Toast bread cutouts on one side and spread untoasted side with mushroom mixture. Sprinkle lightly with paprika and broil until bubbly. May be frozen before broiling.
Makes 6 to 7 dozen

CRAB CANAPES

6 to 7 dozen bread rounds or cutouts
8 ounces cream cheese, softened
1 7-1/2-ounce can minced clams, drained
3/4 cup flaked crab meat
2 teaspoons grated onion
2 tablespoons minced chives
1 teaspoon Worcestershire sauce
1/2 teaspoon each garlic powder and
   white pepper
paprika

Toast bread rounds on one side, flip over and cool. Combine cream cheese, clams, crab, onion, chives, Worcestershire sauce, garlic powder and pepper. Adjust seasonings and spread mixture on untoasted side of bread rounds. Sprinkle with paprika. Broil until bubbly. May be made ahead or may be frozen.
Makes approximately 6 to 7 dozen

TOMATO-CHEESE ROUNDS

3-1/2 to 4-1/2 dozen bread rounds
1/2 cup grated sharp Cheddar cheese
1/3 cup mayonnaise
1/4 cup very finely minced green onions and tops
3 tablespoons very finely minced green pepper
1/8 teaspoon each garlic powder, salt and
   cayenne pepper
mayonnaise for spreading
cherry tomatoes, thinly sliced
bacon
paprika

Toast bread rounds on one side and set aside. Combine cheese, mayonnaise, onion, green pepper and seasonings. Spread untoasted side of bread rounds with mayonnaise, top with a slice of tomato, mound with about 1 teaspoon cheese mixture and top with a tiny piece of bacon. Sprinkle with paprika and broil until bubbly. Cool slightly before serving as the tomato retains heat.
Makes approximately 4 dozen

GORGONZOLA CANAPES

3-1/2 to 4-1/2 dozen slices French bread roll or
   small cocktail rye bread
6 ounces Gorgonzola cheese, crumbled
1/4 pound butter, softened
1/2 teaspoon celery salt
1/3 cup finely chopped pecans
paprika

Toast bread on one side and set aside. Combine cheese, butter, celery salt and pecans. Spread on untoasted side of bread, sprinkle with paprika and broil until bubbly. May be frozen up to 2 weeks before broiling.
Makes approximately 4 dozen

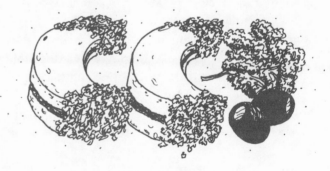

hot canapes

QUICK BREAD IDEAS

• Roll packaged biscuit mix 1/4 inch thick, cut in 4-inch rounds and top with a mixture of 1 cup corned beef hash, 1 tablespoon chili sauce, 1/4 cup minced onion and 1/4 teaspoon pepper. Place 1 tablespoon on circle, fold over and seal edges. Prick top and bake in a 425° oven 12 to 15 minutes.

• Roll packaged crescent rolls 1/4 inch thick. Spread with a mixture of 4 tablespoons each melted butter and minced parsley and 2 table- spoons minced chives. Roll like a jelly roll and seal edges. Form a ring and cut on diagonal almost all the way through. Bake in a 375° oven 15 to 20 minutes.

• Separate packaged butterflake rolls and dip each layer in a mixture of 4 tablespoons melted butter, 1/3 cup minced celery leaves, 1/2 teaspoon sea- soned salt, 1/4 teaspoon celery salt and 1 table- spoon minced parsley. Stand upright in a ring-mold pan and spread with rest of butter and herb mix- ture. Bake in a 375° oven 20 to 30 minutes.

• Cut bread (white, Italian, French or sourdough) in slices almost all the way through. Spread cut slices with: minced onion and garlic sautéed in butter to which is added grated Parmesan cheese, mixed Italian seasoning and minced parsley; or 4 tablespoons softened butter beaten with 2 table- spoons oil and 1/2 teaspoon Worcestershire sauce to which is added 1 pressed garlic clove, 2 table- spoons minced parsley and salt, pepper and paprika to taste and allowed to stand several hours; or 1/4 pound softened butter combined with 1 table- spoon grated onion, 1/2 teaspoon thyme and 1 cup finely grated sharp Cheddar cheese. Wrap loosely in foil and bake in a 375° oven 15 to 20 minutes.

• Mix 1/4 pound softened butter, 1/4 teaspoon garlic powder and 1/2 teaspoon or more beef extract such as Bovril. Spread on sliced French bread rolls or cocktail rye. Broil until crisp and bubbly.

• Mix 4 tablespoons softened butter, 2 table- spoons oil, 1/2 cup finely minced green onions and tops, 2 tablespoons minced parsley, 1 tablespoon sesame seeds, 1 to 2 teaspoons dry mustard, salt and pepper to taste. Spread on sliced French bread rolls or cocktail rye and sprinkle with paprika. Broil until bubbly.

appetizers

cold appetizers

COLD APPETIZER SUGGESTIONS

• Dip apple cubes in lemon juice and thread on bamboo skewer or cocktail pick with a cube of Camembert cheese.

• Marinate honeydew, cantaloupe or pineapple balls or cubes in port wine several hours. Drain and wrap in prosciutto or dried beef.

• Sprinkle fresh figs with pepper and wrap in prosciutto.

• Soak pitted prunes in rum, drain and stuff with softened cream cheese.

• Marinate pitted prunes in sherry 12 hours or more. Drain and insert a small piece of cheese in center.

• Put large pecan halves together with anchovy paste.

• Stuff radish roses with 1 part cream cheese, 2 parts grated Cheddar cheese, and garlic powder and minced chives to taste.

• Roll watercress sprigs in prosciutto.

• Slice young peeled kohlrabi very thinly. Sprinkle with seasoned salt and chill at least 1 hour.

• Place a dab of mustard mayonnaise on the end of a small leaf of Belgian endive or cooked artichoke leaf, top with crab leg or cooked shrimp and another dab of mayonnaise. Arrange in spoke fashion on large round serving platter.

• Form small balls of steak tartare (page 160), garnish with parsley and serve with cocktail picks and dip or sauce of choice.

• Marinate cooked cocktail sausages or cut-up frankfurters in French dressing several hours. Drain, cut lengthwise to make a pocket, spread inside with a little mustard and insert a strip of gherkin.

• Spread thin slices of bologna or other cold cuts with thin layer of softened cream cheese, minced chives, minced parsley and horseradish (optional). Stack 4 at a time, wrap well and chill or freeze. With sharp knife cut into exact squares and pierce each square with a toothpick.

• Skewer tiny pieces of cooked sweetbreads and cherry tomatoes.

• On wooden platter arrange dark bread, slices of goat cheese, walnut halves, green onion lengths and radishes. Garnish with fresh coriander*.

• Sprinkle cream cheese with black sesame seeds or frost with chutney or plum sauce*.

• Skewer a small cube of white cheese and a piece of canned hot green chili pepper. Serve with tortilla chips.

• Pour a generous amount of Worcestershire sauce over block of cream cheese.

• Bind chopped sardines with mayonnaise and add minced onion and dill pickles, lemon juice and Worcestershire sauce to taste.

• Serve raw oysters or clams in the half shell with lemon juice and minced parsley.

*See glossary

ROLL-UPS

Combination of 3-ounce packages (not ripple variety) of pressed chicken, turkey breast, dark turkey, corned beef, pastrami and smoked beef, and thinly sliced ham. (Each package contains from 6 to 11 slices depending upon meat.) Spread with seasoned mayonnaise, cream cheese spread or other fillings that complement the poultry or meat. Sprinkle with minced parsley or watercress, fold over into a triangle and roll from one pointed end. Place seam side down and tuck tiny leaf of parsley, chervil or watercress into small pocket. Arrange spoke fashion on large serving platter and garnish with parsley sprigs and cherry tomatoes.

Filling ideas
• Soften cream cheese with a little cream and season with prepared horseradish; spread on ham and roll.
• Season butter with chicken liver pâté and spread on ham. Sprinkle with minced parsley and roll.
• Combine softened cream cheese and pickle relish to taste. Spread on thinly sliced salami and roll.

CHEESE ROLL-UPS

2 avocados, mashed (about 1 cup)
1 tablespoon lemon juice
1/4 teaspoon each salt and pepper
3 or 4 drops Tabasco
1 cup finely minced cooked shrimp
1 cup finely shredded lettuce
1/4 cup crumbled Gorgonzola cheese
36 thin slices Monterey Jack or mild
   Cheddar cheese

Presentation
shredded lettuce
parsley
shrimp
olives, halved

Combine avocado, lemon juice, seasonings, shrimp, lettuce and Gorgonzola. Adjust seasonings to taste. Have cheese slices at room temperature. Spread with mixture, dividing evenly, and roll like a jelly roll as tightly as possible. Place seam side down on cookie sheet; cover and refrigerate.
To serve arrange rolls spoke fashion on lettuce. Garnish with parsley, shrimp and olives.
Makes 3 dozen

cold appetizers

LOX ROLL-UPS

1 pound lox, thinly sliced
8 ounces cream cheese
2 tablespoons cream
1/2 teaspoon onion powder
1/4 teaspoon garlic powder
1/2 teaspoon grated lemon peel
2 teaspoons dill weed
tiny parsley sprigs
tiny slices of lemon

Cut lox into rectangles approximately 1-1/2x2-1/2 inches. Combine cheese, cream, onion and garlic powder, lemon peel and dill. Spread on lox, roll, trim ends and arrange seam side down on serving plate. Garnish each roll with a tiny parsley sprig and a tiny slice of lemon.
Makes approximately 3-1/2 dozen

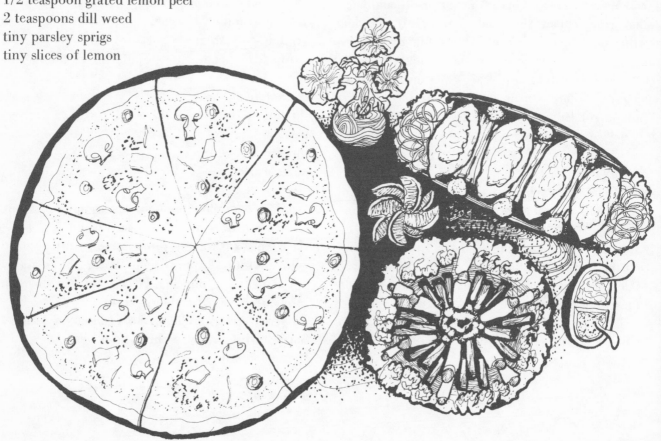

SHRIMP BOWL

2 pounds raw shrimp
1/2 cup lemon juice
1/4 cup chopped onion
1 tablespoon minced fresh dill weed
1 teaspoon each salt and sugar
1/4 teaspoon each allspice and nutmeg

Presentation
lemon wedges
avocado balls
parsley sprigs

Boil shrimp in salted water until just pink. Drain and reserve cooking water. When cool, shell and devein. Combine remaining ingredients with 1 cup cooking water and marinate shrimp 8 hours or overnight. Drain.
To serve mound shrimp in bowl nested in ice. Garnish with lemon wedges, avocado balls and parsley. Serve with cracker or bread of choice.
Makes 30 to 40 buffet servings

ANTIPASTO ROUNDS

12 slices Monterey Jack cheese
36 oval slices Italian dry salami
1 7-ounce can tuna, drained and flaked
2 hard-cooked eggs, chopped
1/2 cup mayonnaise
2 or 3 drained and chopped pepperoncini
36 stuffed green olives

Cut each cheese slice into thirds. Arrange a cheese slice on top of each slice of salami. Combine tuna, eggs, mayonnaise and pepperoncini. Spread about 1 tablespoon of the mixture over cheese. Place an olive at the edge of the tuna mixture and roll the salami around olive, jelly-roll fashion. Secure with a toothpick.
Makes 36 rolls

cold appetizers

ANTIPASTO

2/3 cup olive oil
1/4 cup wine vinegar
1 tablespoon finely minced fresh basil or
   1 teaspoon dried basil
1 clove garlic, finely minced
1/2 teaspoon salt
freshly ground black pepper
1/4 cup finely chopped parsley
1 10-ounce package frozen artichoke halves,
   cooked and drained
1 16-ounce can garbanzo beans
1/2 pound tiny mushroom caps
1 7-ounce can tuna, drained

Combine oil, vinegar, basil, garlic, salt, pepper and parsley. Shake until well blended. Pour oil and vinegar mixture over remaining ingredients; toss to coat well. Chill several hours or overnight.

Presentation suggestions
1 large head romaine lettuce
dry Italian salami, thinly sliced
sliced prosciutto or Westphalian ham
mortadella, sliced
head cheese, sliced
pickled pigs' feet
coppa (cured pork with red pepper), sliced
shrimp with tails on, cooked, cleaned and chilled
anchovy fillets with capers
sardines in oil
smoked oysters
Provolone cheese, cubed
ricotta cheese
Mozzarella cheese, cubed
hard-cooked eggs, quartered
large green olives
large black olives
radish roses
celery sticks
green onions
fresh fennel
cherry tomatoes
caponatina, canned (marinated eggplant mixture)
pepperoncini
green pepper, cut in strips
pimiento, cut in strips

Shred romaine and arrange in the center of a large platter. Spoon chilled vegetable and tuna mixture into center of lettuce. Surround with your choice of suggestions.

SASHIMI

fresh fish or shellfish of choice
daikon* finely shredded into long strands
finely shredded carrot
chrysanthemum leaves and flowers
ivy or maple leaves
shredded cabbage, cucumber or turnip
parsley sprigs
turnip chrysanthemum
thin lemon wedges
wasabi*
finely minced ginger root

Dipping Sauces
• For white-meat fish use soy sauce diluted with sake or dry sherry and a little rice vinegar*.
• For other fish or shellfish combine equal parts soy sauce and lime juice. Or simmer 1 cup soy sauce with 2 tablespoons sake or dry sherry, 1 teaspoon sugar and a pinch katsuobushi* 10 minutes. Strain.

*See glossary

A perfect beginning for a special dinner, light and appealing to the eye. Use only the freshest fish or shellfish, *never* frozen fish. The tunas (excluding albacore), the marlins, porgies, bass and snappers, bonito and other firm fish can be eaten raw according to the season. Keep fish as cold as possible and rinse your hands in ice water often to prevent their warmth from damaging the fish. Cut fish across the grain into bite-sized slices approximately 1/4 inch thick. Slice shrimp and cut squid, crab, abalone and lobster into threadlike slices.

Cover chilled serving platter with daikon and a border of carrot. Arrange fish in overlapping slices on daikon and garnish with chrysanthemum leaves and flowers, ivy or maple leaves, shredded cabbage, cucumber or turnip, parsley and/or turnip chrysanthemum. In separate dishes place the lemon wedges, wasabi and ginger root. Place one of the dipping sauce or sauces in small bowls.

Guests help themselves with chopsticks or forks and dip fish pieces into sauce and then wasabi and/or ginger root.

cold appetizers

STUFFED SHRIMP

3 ounces cream cheese, softened
1/4 cup crumbled blue cheese
1/2 teaspoon dry mustard
1 tablespoon chopped parsley
1 green onion, chopped
1 4-ounce can chopped black olives
36 large cooked and cleaned prawns
36 small cherry tomatoes

Blend cream cheese, blue cheese, mustard, parsley, onion and chopped olives. Split prawns halfway through (butterfly fashion) and stuff with cheese mixture. Chill. Just before serving spear a cherry tomato into each shrimp with short skewer.
Makes 36

Variations
Stuff with horseradish butter and roll curve of filling in finely minced chives or parsley. Or stuff with mixture of cream cheese, finely chopped walnuts and sieved hard-cooked eggs; roll in chopped watercress.

STUFFED CELERY STALKS

12 celery stalks (washed and trimmed)
5 sprigs fresh parsley
2 hard-cooked eggs
2 tablespoons mayonnaise
salt and white pepper
1 3-3/4-ounce can Norway sardines

Chop into very fine dice, 1 celery stalk, the parsley and hard-cooked eggs. Combine with mayonnaise. Season mixture to taste with salt and white pepper. Cut remaining celery stalks into 2- or 3-inch strips. Using a pastry bag and large point or a teaspoon, stuff each celery stalk with prepared mixture. Top with 1 whole sardine.
Makes about 22 servings

Stuffed Celery Variations
• Combine softened cream cheese, minced black olives, chopped cashews or other nuts, Worcestershire sauce and onion powder to taste.
• Combine 4 ounces cream cheese, 2 tablespoons butter, 12 anchovies, minced, 1 teaspoon or more lemon juice.
• Combine cream cheese, mayonnaise, finely chopped cooked or canned shrimp, minced onion, parsley, celery, green olives and/or green pepper, Worcestershire sauce, Tabasco, salt and pepper.
• Combine cream cheese, crumbled blue cheese, parsley and chives, tomato paste, garlic salt, Tabasco.
• Stuff with mock liver pâté (page 77).

STUFFED CHERRY TOMATOES

Cut a tiny slice from top of tomato, scoop out pulp with small spoon and turn upside down on rack to drain. Stem end serves as a flat bottom so tomatoes will stand upright. A cup filling will stuff 40 to 50 tomatoes. Serve chilled.

• Hard-cooked egg yolks, mashed and seasoned to taste with anchovy paste, minced capers and ripe olives, prepared mustard, brandy and olive oil and enough mayonnaise to make creamy. Top with tiny olive slice.

• Canned salmon or tuna seasoned to taste with chili sauce, grated onion, dill weed, Worcestershire, lemon juice, salt and Tabasco and enough mayonnaise to make creamy. Top with tiny parsley leaf.

• Mash avocado and season with lemon juice, grated onion, salt and pepper and mayonnaise to make creamy. Top with bit of cooked crumbled bacon.

• Combine 1/4 cup softened butter and 2 sieved hard-cooked egg yolks. Season to taste with anchovy paste, garlic powder, minced parsley and minced chives. Roll filled top in minced parsley.

• Mash equal parts cream cheese and Gorgonzola cheese and season to taste with grated onion or minced chives. Top with tiny sliver of black olive.

• Cream softened cream cheese with minced shrimp, Worcestershire sauce and Tabasco to taste. Top with tiny feather of dill.

• Wash and drain sauerkraut. Stuff generously so filling makes a mound.

• Jellied consommé or aspic topped with dab of sour cream.

• Smoked oyster topped with parsley leaf.

• Softened cream cheese, minced celery, dill weed, onion and garlic powder, chives and parsley. Top with celery leaf.

FILLED BEETS

Cut small slice off tops of tiny canned beets. Hollow them out and fill with mixtures suggested below. Serve well chilled.

• Chopped hard-cooked egg, mashed sardines or anchovies, minced capers and gherkins. Top with parsley leaf.

• Chopped watercress, minced celery, sieved hard-cooked eggs, mayonnaise, salt, curry powder, Tabasco. Top with watercress sprig.

• 1/4 cup heavy cream, whipped, 3 sieved hard-cooked eggs, anchovy paste and mayonnaise. Top with parsley leaf.

• See stuffings for tomatoes.

cold appetizers

FILLED RAW MUSHROOMS

Serve either completely raw or if desired poach 3 minutes in 2 cups water and 1 tablespoon lemon juice. Drain and dry. Brush raw or poached mushroom caps with lemon juice inside and out before filling. Following are fillings for 24 medium mushrooms (1-1/2 inches in diameter), about 1 pound.

• Mash 4 ounces Gorgonzola cheese, 3 ounces cream cheese and 2 tablespoons butter. Season to taste with grated onion, salt and Worcestershire sauce. Fill and top with minced green pepper. Chill before serving.

• Mash 5 ounces Gorgonzola cheese and blend in 2 tablespoons sour cream and 1 teaspoon minced chives. Add brandy to taste. Fill and sprinkle with paprika. Chill.

• Combine 4 ounces cream cheese with just enough sour cream to soften. Season to taste with lemon juice and white pepper. Fill just to rim; top with red caviar and a tiny lemon peel. Chill.

• Combine 1/4 pound finely minced lox and 4 ounces cream cheese with grated lemon peel and dill weed. Fill and sprinkle with paprika. Chill.

• Sauté 1 cup bread crumbs seasoned to taste in 2 tablespoons butter. Fill and sprinkle with minced parsley and chives. Serve at room temperature.

• Fill with pâté and top with crumbled cooked bacon or chopped pistachio nuts. Serve at room temperature.

• Fill with lumpfish caviar, sprinkle with lemon juice and garnish with sieved hard-cooked egg yolk and tiny parsley leaf. Sprinkle with paprika and chill before serving.

• Season 3/4 cup ricotta cheese to taste with salt, curry powder, grated onion and minced chives. Fill and sprinkle with paprika. Chill.

STUFFED EGGS

Hard-boil 14 small eggs. Halve and push yolks through medium sieve. Combine yolks with the following suggested fillings and mound mixture in egg-white halves. If piping, reserve yolks of 5 eggs and mix with mayonnaise to make right consistency to use in pastry tube. After filling, decorate as desired. Eggs can be cooked a day ahead and filled the day of the party. Place on wax paper in a glass pan with sides, cover with saran wrap and refrigerate. Always adjust fillings to taste and sprinkle with paprika if color is needed.

• Mix sieved yolks with 1/2 cup chicken liver pâté with mushrooms (page 74). Decorate with thin slices of ripe olive.

• Mix sieved yolks with 2 tablespoons soft butter, 1/2 teaspoon each dry mustard and salt, 1/4 teaspoon white pepper and herb mayonnaise to moisten. Sprinkle with paprika and top with a cooked baby shrimp and a tiny parsley leaf.

- Mix sieved egg yolks with 1 to 2 teaspoons curry powder, 1 teaspoon soy sauce, 1 to 2 teaspoons lemon juice, mayonnaise to moisten and white pepper to taste. Top with tiny piece of chutney.
- Mix sieved egg yolks with 1/2 cup minced olives, salt, pepper and dry mustard (optional) to taste and mayonnaise to moisten. Sprinkle with paprika.
- Mix sieved egg yolks with 1/4 cup chili sauce, 1 tablespoon minced parsley, 3 tablespoons finely minced green onion and tops, 2 tablespoons finely minced celery, salt, pepper and Dijon-style mustard to taste, mayonnaise to moisten if needed. Garnish with tiny celery leaf.
- Mix sieved egg yolks with 1/4 cup sour cream or yoghurt, 2 tablespoons finely minced pimiento-stuffed olives, 1 tablespoon each minced parsley, chives and celery; add salt, pepper and Dijon-style mustard to taste. Top with tiny sliver of green pepper.
- Mix sieved egg yolks with 3/4 cup finely minced raw mushrooms, lemon juice, oregano, white pepper and salt to taste, mayonnaise to moisten. Top with watercress.
- Mix sieved egg yolks with chili powder, basil, cumin, turmeric or curry to taste, mayonnaise to moisten. Top with tiny slice of cherry tomato.
- Mix sieved egg yolks with 2 tablespoons soft butter, 2 to 3 tablespoons chopped pimientos, salt and white pepper to taste, mayonnaise to moisten. Top with watercress.
- Mix sieved yolks with 1/2 cup béarnaise sauce. Top with tiny watercress sprig.
- Mix sieved yolks with 2/3 cup sour cream, salt and white pepper to taste. Decorate with a tiny lemon slice and a dab of lumpfish caviar.
- Mix sieved yolks with 1/2 cup lumpfish caviar, dry mustard, Worcestershire sauce and white pepper to taste, plus homemade mayonnaise to moisten. Top with sliver of lemon rind.
- Mix sieved yolks with 1/2 cup grated Gruyère cheese, 5 tablespoons soft butter, salt, pepper and Tabasco to taste. Decorate with tiny strips of Gruyère cheese.
- Sauté 1 cup finely minced sorrel and 3 tablespoons minced shallots in 4 tablespoons butter. Cool, mix with sieved yolks and season to taste with salt, pepper and lemon juice. Top with tiny parsley leaf.
- Mix sieved egg yolks with 1/2 cup mushroom duxelle (page 12) and sour cream if needed to moisten. Top with dab of sour cream and tiny parsley leaf. Sprinkle with paprika.
- Purée in blender: 2/3 cup smoked oysters, 2 tablespoons chopped green onion and 2 tablespoons soft butter. Stir in sieved egg yolks, 2 tablespoons minced parsley, mayonnaise to moisten and salt, pepper, garlic powder and curry powder to taste. Sprinkle with paprika and decorate with ripe olive halves.

cold appetizers

FILLED ARTICHOKE BOTTOMS

Drain marinated artichoke bottoms and reserve marinade for sautéing. Dry artichoke bottoms and sprinkle with salt, white pepper, paprika and lemon juice. Mound filling and garnish.

• Cream cheese, paprika, cream to soften. Top with lumpfish caviar, tiny lemon peel and parsley leaf.

• Chicken liver pâté (page 74) or mock liver pâté (page 77).

• Fillings for small tarts (page 120).

• Creamed spinach: Combine 1 package frozen chopped spinach cooked dry, 1/2 recipe velouté sauce, grated onion and garlic, salt and pepper to taste. Mound, sprinkle with paprika and bake in 350° oven 10 to 15 minutes to heat through. Garnish with sieved hard-cooked egg. (This is also good with poached zucchini boats.)

DOLMAS

Recipes are for 1 12-ounce jar grape leaves preserved in brine. Grape leaves directly from the vine may also be used. Unfold leaves and rinse first in cold then in hot water. Pat dry and spread out shiny side down. Remove tough stem ends and place 2 teaspoons or more filling on stem end. Fold in sides and roll tightly toward tip. If leaves are very large or if small buffet-size dolmas are preferred, halve the leaves before filling and rolling. Put a 1/4-inch layer of olive oil in a large kettle. Arrange dolmas closely in kettle seam side down. Tuck small parsley sprigs between them and weight down with a heavy plate. Pour in 1-3/4 cup beef stock or 1 10-1/2-ounce can consommé diluted with 1/2 cup water and 2 to 3 tablespoons lemon juice. Cover kettle, bring to gentle boil and cook, adding liquid if needed, 25 minutes for large dolmas, 15 to 20 minutes for small. Transfer to chafing dish. There should be approximately 1 cup liquid left in kettle. Pour over dolmas and serve with yoghurt sauce or tomato sauce.
Makes approximately 30 large, 50 small

• *Variations:* Add 1/2 cup sour cream or tomato purée to juices. Or beat 2 egg yolks, gradually add to reserved liquid and beat constantly until thickened. Pour over dolmas.

• *Lamb Filling* Combine 1 pound lean ground lamb, 1/4 cup minced onion, 1 teaspoon pressed garlic, 2 tablespoons each minced parsley and mint or fresh dill weed, 1/2 teaspoon each salt, pepper, oregano and thyme, 1 .cup minced peeled and seeded tomatoes, 2 tablespoons tomato paste and 1/4 cup chopped pine nuts (optional). Adjust for seasonings.

• *Rice Filling* Soak 1/4 cup currants in 2 tablespoons dry white wine 1 hour; drain. In 1/4 cup olive oil, sauté 1 cup minced onion with 1/2 teaspoon salt and 1/4 teaspoon pepper until transparent. Add 1 cup washed and drained raw rice, 1-1/2 cups water and 2 tablespoons lemon juice. Bring to gentle boil and cook until rice is almost tender, adding more liquid if needed. Add currants and 1/4 cup minced parsley, 3 tablespoons chopped pine nuts, 1 tablespoon chopped mint, 1-1/2 teaspoons minced oregano, 1/2 teaspoon salt and 1/4 teaspoon each allspice and cinnamon. Adjust seasonings to taste.

• *Pork and Beef Filling* Combine 1 pound lean ground beef, 1/2 pound lean ground pork, 3/4 cup minced onion, 1/2 cup minced parsley, 1-1/2 tablespoons lemon juice, 3/4 teaspoon each salt, minced marjoram and minced basil and 1/4 teaspoon pepper. Adjust seasonings and add 1 cup washed and drained raw rice.

cold appetizers

SUSHI

Rice

3 cups pearl rice (short grain)
water to cover
1 tablespoon sake or dry sherry
3 cups boiling water
1 3-inch piece kombu*, broken into
    several pieces (optional)
1/3 cup rice vinegar*
2 tablespoons sugar
1 teaspoon toasted sesame seeds (optional)

*See glossary

Wash rice in at least 8 changes of water until washing water is clear. Cover with water and let stand 30 minutes. Drain. Add sake to boiling water and gradually stir in rice. Top with kombu, cover tightly and cook on high heat until rice starts to steam over. Lower heat to medium and cook 6 minutes. Turn off heat and let stand 20 minutes. Discard kombu and turn rice into large wooden bowl (wood absorbs moisture).

Combine vinegar, sugar and sesame seeds and quickly pour over hot rice, fanning to cool so rice doesn't get soggy. When cool enough to handle, form into desired shapes and top with foods of choice according to following suggestions.

Toppings

cooked poultry or meat, cut into small strips
tiny bits of raw fish
tiny cooked shrimp or other seafood
green peas or beans cooked tender-crisp
carrots and/or cucumbers cut in tiny strips
pickled red ginger* cut in tiny strips
egg garni*, plain or made with 2 ounces fillet
　　of sole, minced
dried forest mushrooms* softened, slivered and
　　cooked in stock
slivers of ginger root
nori*
matsuba*
wasabi*
marinated raw vegetables
watercress

*See glossary

Presentation Suggestions

• Shape 1 or 2 tablespoons rice mixture into ovals, squares or circles. Garnish with food of choice or cover completely with, for example, a piece of thinly sliced raw fish and then garnish.

• Arrange thin slices of cucumber in a square pan, fill with rice and pat down. Let stand until completely cool and caked; then invert on board. Cut into squares or diamonds and garnish as desired.

• Mix minced garnish choices in with the rice. Trim edges of uncut egg garni to make a 5-inch square. Form 3 tablespoons of rice mixture into a square and place on center of egg garni. Wrap and place seam side down. Garnish with a strip of nori and preserved ginger or other garnish.

• Lightly toast nori over flame or in hot skillet. Place on sudare (a 9x9-inch bamboo mat available in Oriental shops), or heavy cloth napkin and spread with rice, leaving a 1-inch border on bottom and top. Arrange garnishes such as softened mushrooms, egg garni, watercress or matsuba and shrimp on top. Roll firmly like a jelly roll and chill 10 minutes. Unroll, trim ends and with a very sharp knife cut into 6 to 8 slices. Arrange cut side up in groups of threes to resemble a flower.

cold appetizers

GORGONZOLA BALLS

6 ounces cream cheese
2 ounces Gorgonzola cheese, crumbled
2 tablespoons each finely minced celery
   and parsley
1 tablespoon finely minced onion
salt, white pepper and cayenne pepper to taste
mayonnaise if too stiff
finely chopped walnuts

Combine all ingredients except walnuts. Chill, form
into balls and shortly before serving roll in walnuts.
Makes approximately 3 dozen 3/4-inch balls

CHUTNEY-CHICKEN BALLS

1/4 to 1/3 cup finely chopped chutney
1 5-ounce can chicken spread
salt, white pepper and curry powder to taste
finely chopped almonds

Combine all ingredients except almonds. Chill,
form into balls and shortly before serving roll in
almonds.
Makes approximately 2 dozen 3/4-inch balls

CLAM-VEAL BALLS

6 ounces cream cheese
1 7-1/2-ounce can minced clams, drained
1-1/2 cups ground cooked veal
1 teaspoon each lemon juice and paprika
salt, white pepper, garlic powder and
   anchovy paste to taste
finely minced parsley

Combine all ingredients except parsley. Chill, form
into balls and chill until shortly before serving.
Roll in parsley.
Makes approximately 4 dozen 3/4-inch balls

ALMOND-CHICKEN BALLS

8 ounces cream cheese
1 cup ground cooked chicken
3/4 cup finely chopped blanched almonds
2 tablespoons mayonnaise
curry powder, salt, white pepper and
   chopped chutney to taste
finely grated coconut

Combine all ingredients except coconut. Chill,
form into balls, roll in coconut and chill until
ready to serve.
Makes approximately 4 dozen 3/4-inch balls

HAM AND EGG BALLS

equal amounts of ground cooked ham and
   sieved hard-cooked eggs
salt and white pepper to taste
mustard to taste
mayonnaise to bind
drained capers

Combine all ingredients except capers. Chill and
form into balls. Flatten slightly and press 1 or 2
capers in center. Refrigerate until ready to serve.

SHRIMP BALLS

1 pound ground, cooked shrimp
1 tablespoon chili sauce
1/4 cup very finely minced celery
2 tablespoons very finely minced water chestnuts
1-1/2 tablespoons grated onion
1 hard-cooked egg, sieved
3 ounces cream cheese, softened
1/2 teaspoon salt
1/8 teaspoon white pepper
1/16 teaspoon cayenne pepper
1 teaspoon lemon juice
minced parsley

Combine all ingredients except parsley and adjust
seasonings. Chill. Form into 1-inch balls and roll in
minced parsley.
Makes approximately 50 3/4-inch balls

CHEDDAR-CHILI BALLS

6 ounces Cheddar cheese, grated
2 ounces cream cheese
pressed garlic to taste
chili powder

Combine cheeses and garlic. Chill, form into balls
and roll in chili powder. Keep refrigerated until
ready to serve.
Makes approximately 2 dozen 3/4-inch balls

CHEDDAR-OLIVE BALLS

1/4 pound Cheddar cheese, grated
1 4-ounce can chopped black olives
2 tablespoons softened butter
pressed garlic, curry powder and Tabasco to taste
black olive slivers

Combine all ingredients except olive slivers. Chill,
form into balls and garnish each with olive sliver.
Refrigerate until ready to serve.
Makes approximately 2 dozen 3/4-inch balls

hot appetizers

HOT APPETIZER SUGGESTIONS

• Wrap bacon slices around Waverly wafers. Bake in a 350° oven 10 minutes or until bacon is crisp. Drain and place on paper toweling. Cool slightly before serving. May be made ahead and refrigerated or frozen. Reheat in 350° oven.

• Fry shrimp chips in deep oil 8 seconds or until puffed. Serve with dip of cream cheese softened with sour cream and seasoned to taste with chopped chutney and curry powder.

• Dip shelled, deveined shrimp in garlic olive oil* and seasoned bread crumbs. Bake in 400° oven 5 minutes and broil to crisp.

• Have butcher saw marrow bones into 1-inch pieces. Wipe with damp cloth and place on baking sheet. Broil 3 to 5 minutes until center of marrow is barely brown. Serve as spread for French bread.

*See glossary

RUMAKI

Wrap slightly sautéed bacon around suggestions below, secure with toothpicks and broil until bacon is crisp.

• Chicken livers and/or water chestnuts, marinated if desired.

• Chicken livers wrapped around small piece of sweet gherkin.

• Pitted prunes stuffed with pecan halves.

• Pitted dates stuffed with pineapple or Monterey Jack cheese.

• Pitted dates marinated in brandy or sherry and stuffed with piece of water chestnut.

• Shrimp sprinkled with powdered ginger and pepper or cayenne pepper.

• Shrimp or cooked sweetbreads marinated in mixture of 1/2 cup each white wine and chili sauce, 3 tablespoons oil, 1 teaspoon minced tarragon and 2 teaspoons minced parsley. Use as dip as well as marinade.

• Pitted ripe olives stuffed with sharp Cheddar cheese.

• Anchovy or pecan-stuffed olives marinated in dry vermouth.

• Small raw mushroom caps sprinkled with oregano and lemon juice.

• Drained canned shad roe, cut in cubes.

• Fresh figs.

• Oysters drained and patted dry, then sprinkled with lemon juice, and Tabasco and bit of pimiento.

• Orange sections or pineapple or apple chunks.

• Cubes of cooked veal and Swiss cheese.

HOT STUFFED MUSHROOMS

16 to 24 large mushrooms
1-1/2 tablespoons butter, melted
2 tablespoons finely minced onion
1/4 teaspoon finely minced garlic (optional)
3 tablespoons butter
paprika
one of following stuffings

Remove mushroom stems. Brush caps with melted butter and set aside. Finely chop stems and sauté with onion and optional garlic in butter. Combine with one of the stuffings below and adjust seasonings to taste. Fill caps and sprinkle with paprika. Place in well-buttered shallow baking dish and bake in a 400° oven 10 to 15 minutes until mushrooms are tender and tops are browned. Garnish first 3 stuffings with small parsley sprig, ham with black olive half.

• *Walnut Stuffing:* Combine sautéed stems with 1 cup fine bread crumbs, 1/4 cup grated Parmesan cheese, 3 tablespoons finely chopped walnuts, 2 teaspoons Worcestershire sauce, 1/2 teaspoon salt, 1/4 teaspoon pepper and chicken or beef stock to moisten.

• *Almond Stuffing:* Combine sautéed stems with 1/4 cup toasted slivered almonds, crushed, 1/4 cup each fine bread crumbs and herb mayonnaise and 1/4 cup grated Monterey Jack or mild Cheddar cheese. Top with 1/4 cup toasted slivered almonds, crushed.

• *Crab Stuffing:* Combine sautéed stems with 1/2 pound crab meat, cooked and flaked, 2 eggs, lightly beaten, 2 tablespoons each soft bread crumbs, mayonnaise and finely chopped green onion, 1 teaspoon lemon juice, 1/8 teaspoon each salt, cayenne pepper and oregano. Top with 2 tablespoons soft bread crumbs mixed with 2 tablespoons melted butter.

• *Ham Stuffing:* Combine sautéed stems with 1-1/2 cups ground cooked ham, 1/2 cup sour cream, 2 tablespoons each minced parsley and chives and 1/4 teaspoon each salt and pepper.

• *Shrimp Stuffing:* Combine sautéed stems with 1 pound minced cooked shrimp, 1 beaten egg, 1/4 cup fine bread crumbs, 1 tablespoon each lemon juice, minced green onion and minced parsley, 1/2 teaspoon salt, 1/4 teaspoon white pepper and 3 tablespoons melted butter or more to moisten. After baking, cover each mushroom with 2 tablespoons mornay sauce, top each with a whole cooked shrimp and broil to heat. Garnish with parsley.

hot appetizers

DEEP-FRIED CHEESE BALLS

3 cups grated Cheddar cheese
2 tablespoons flour
3/4 teaspoon salt
1/16 teaspoon cayenne pepper
4 egg whites, stiffly beaten
cracker crumbs
shortening for deep frying

Mix together cheese, flour, salt and cayenne. Fold in beaten egg whites. Form with fingers into 1-inch balls and roll in cracker crumbs. Deep fry a few at a time draining on paper toweling as they are cooked. Serve with toothpicks.
These may be prepared 1 or 2 hours in advance and stored, uncooked, in the refrigerator.
Makes approximately 4 dozen

BROILED MARINATED SHRIMP

3/4 cup each olive oil and sherry
2 tablespoons minced parsley
1 tablespoon minced chives
1 teaspoon each minced garlic,
    tarragon and chervil
1/2 teaspoon salt
1/4 teaspoon white pepper
3 pounds medium shrimp, shelled and deveined

Combine ingredients and marinate shrimp 4 to 6 hours, turning often. Remove from marinade and brush off any large bits of garlic or herbs. Place in shallow baking pan in single layer and broil to brown lightly, basting with strained marinade. Turn and broil other side. Serve with melba rounds.
Makes approximately 45

Variation
Omit tarragon and chervil. Add 1/2 teaspoon crushed dried red pepper and 2 to 3 tablespoons mustard.

DEEP-FRIED SHRIMP TRIANGLES

16 slices 1- or 2-day-old white bread
1 or 2 egg whites, slightly beaten
1 recipe shrimp balls (page 61)
about 3/4 cup sesame seeds
peanut or corn oil

Remove crusts from bread and toast in 250° oven
15 minutes. Brush with egg white and spread with
shrimp mixture. Sprinkle with sesame seeds and
lower spread side down 2 slices at a time into hot
oil. Deep fry about 3 minutes or until golden, turn
to brown other side and drain on paper toweling.
Cut into triangles and serve immediately; or keep
warm for several minutes in 350° oven while frying
rest of triangles.
Makes approximately 64 triangles

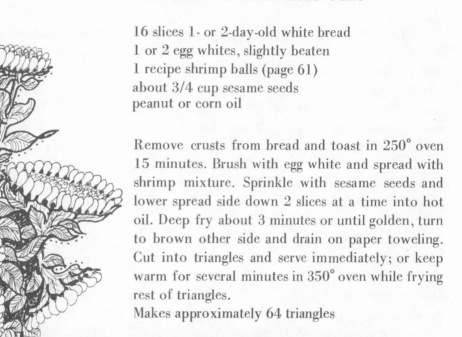

hot appetizers

TOAST CUPS

To make cups: Cut 2-1/2-inch rounds out of thin-sliced white bread. Press round down into well-buttered tiny muffin tins and bake in a 375° oven 10 minutes or until just golden. Fill each with 2 teaspoons of one of the following fillings, top and bake in a 375° oven until bubbly. May be frozen before baking. Allow 1-1/2 cups filling for 3 dozen toast cups.
• Mushroom duxelle (page 12); top each with 1/2 teaspoon grated Parmesan or Cheddar cheese.
• Tomato-ham duxelle (page 12); top each with 1/2 teaspoon grated Parmesan or Cheddar cheese.
• Combine 8 ounces cream cheese, 1 pound flaked crab meat, 2 beaten eggs, 1/4 cup mayonnaise, 3 tablespoons minced parsley.
• Any coquille mixtures, fillings for hot choux or fillings for pastries or phyllo pastries.

CRESCENT ROLL APPETIZERS

Lay crescent roll triangles on board and press 2 together to make a rectangle.
• With pastry wheel cut into 2 lengthwise and 8 crosswise strips. Twist each strip to make a bow. Brush with 1 egg beaten with 1 tablespoon water, sprinkle with grated Parmesan cheese and paprika. Bake in a 375° oven 6 minutes or until golden.
• Spread rectangle with mushroom purée and sprinkle with finely grated Cheddar cheese. Starting from long side, roll like jelly roll. Cut into 3/4-inch rounds and place in tiny buttered muffin tins. Bake in 375° oven 8 to 10 minutes.
• Spread triangle with filling for hot rolled sandwiches; starting from long side, roll like jelly roll. Cut into 1-1/2-inch pieces, brush with 1 egg beaten with 1 tablespoon water and bake in 375° oven 10 to 12 minutes.
• Spread half the rectangle with above filling, fold other half over and seal edges. Cut into small rectangles, brush with 1 egg beaten with 1 tablespoon water and sprinkle with sesame seeds, poppy seeds or chopped almonds. Bake as preceding.

DIP SUGGESTIONS

Serve any of the following combinations with crackers, potato chips, tortilla chips, raw vegetables, etc.
• Lemon Dill* mixed to taste with sour cream. Sprinkle with extra dill, preferably fresh.
• Cream cheese, chopped radishes, salt, lemon juice, dill weed and garlic powder.
• 1/2 pint sour cream, 1/2 cup minced peeled and seeded tomatoes, 2 tablespoons each minced green onions and tops, celery and parsley, 1 tablespoon minced green pepper; salt, white pepper and Tabasco to taste.
• Cream cheese, grated onion, dill weed, salt and white pepper; soften to right consistency with cream.
• Cream cheese, cucumber (minced, salted, drained and dried), minced chives and parsley, grated onion, salt and white pepper.

*See glossary

CUCUMBER DIP

1 small cucumber, peeled, seeded and minced
1/2 teaspoon salt
1/2 pint sour cream
2 tablespoons minced chives
1 tablespoon each lemon juice and
    minced fresh dill weed
1/4 teaspoon white pepper
paprika for garnish

Sprinkle cucumber with salt and toss to mix. Let stand 1 hour and put in strainer to drain. Combine with rest of ingredients and chill. Adjust seasonings and sprinkle with paprika.
Makes 1-1/2 cups

SPINACH DIP

1 10-1/2-ounce package frozen spinach
2 cups plain yoghurt
1 teaspoon pressed garlic
1-1/2 teaspoons lime or lemon juice
1/2 teaspoon salt
1/4 teaspoon each pepper and paprika
1/8 teaspoon cayenne pepper

Cook spinach, drain and press out *all* moisture; chop very finely and chill. Combine with rest of ingredients and adjust to taste.

dips

ZUCCHINI DIP

2 cups diced zucchini
2 tablespoons chopped onion
1/2 teaspoon minced garlic
1/2 teaspoon each salt and paprika
1/4 teaspoon each pepper and basil
8 ounces cream cheese, cubed and softened
1/4 teaspoon Worcestershire sauce
1 teaspoon lemon juice
1/2 teaspoon Sallie's Salt*
paprika and minced parsley for garnish

*See glossary

Combine zucchini, onion, garlic and seasonings; cover and cook 20 minutes until soft. Cool and purée in blender. Add cream cheese and blend. Season with Worcestershire sauce, lemon juice and Sallie's Salt to taste. Chill. Just before serving sprinkle with paprika and parsley.
Makes approximately 2-1/2 cups

PEPPERCORN DIP

29 peppercorns
1 large garlic clove
1/3 cup prepared mustard
2 2-ounce cans anchovy fillets and oil
2 eggs
2 cups salad oil

Blend peppercorns, garlic, mustard and anchovies and their oil in blender. Add 1 egg and blend 1 minute; then slowly blend in 1 cup oil. Repeat process with remaining egg and oil. Serve with crisp raw vegetables.
Makes approximately 3 cups

CLAM DIP

8 ounces cream cheese, softened
1/2 cup sour cream
2 tablespoons mayonnaise
3 dashes Tabasco
1 tablespoon finely grated onion
2 tablespoons chopped pimiento (optional)
2 tablespoons fresh minced dill weed
1 7-ounce can minced clams, drained

Combine all ingredients except clams until very smooth and well blended. Add clams.
Makes 2-1/2 cups

CELERY SEED DIP

1/2 pint sour cream
2 tablespoons tarragon vinegar
1/2 teaspoon salt
1/4 teaspoon white pepper
2 teaspoons celery seeds
paprika

Combine sour cream, vinegar, salt, pepper and celery seeds. Adjust to taste and chill. Sprinkle with paprika just before serving.
Makes 1 cup

GUACAMOLE

2 ripe avocados
2 tablespoons lime or lemon juice
2 teaspoons grated onion
1/2 teaspoon grated garlic
3/4 teaspoon salt
1/4 teaspoon white pepper
1/8 teaspoon each cumin and chili powder
1/3 cup peeled, seeded and finely
   chopped ripe tomatoes
paprika for garnish

Mash avocados with lime or lemon juice. Add remaining ingredients and adjust seasonings to taste. Chill. Just before serving sprinkle with paprika. Serve with tortilla chips.
Makes approximately 2 cups

CHICKEN DIP

3 ounces mushrooms
1 tablespoon butter
1 5-ounce jar boned chicken
1/2 pint sour cream
2 to 3 teaspoons curry powder
1 to 2 tablespoons lemon juice
salt and white pepper to taste
1/2 cup finely chopped cashews or almonds
paprika
minced parsley

Sauté mushrooms in butter until soft. Put in blender with chicken, sour cream and curry. Purée and add lemon juice. Adjust seasonings with salt and white pepper. Just before serving add cashews and pour into serving bowl. Chill. Sprinkle with paprika and minced parsley.
Makes approximately 2 cups

molds
terrines
pates
galantines

MOLDS

Choosing the mold form can be crucial. The form can be deep or shallow depending upon the mold's stiffness and weight of ingredients. It can be shaped like a fish or a fruit or a chicken, or be a fluted pie tin, baking pan, or bowl. Metal containers without intricate designs, sharp corners, or ridges are better than glass, plastic and ceramic because they permit quick cooling and warming of the mold's surface without ruining its shape.

Rinse container in ice water. Fill, decorate, cover and refrigerate 6 hours or overnight. To unmold, hold container in hot water up to the rim *just* until edge starts to melt. Then remove from water and dry outside with towel. Run knife or spatula lightly around the edge to help release the mold. Place chilled plate or platter on top, quickly invert, and give a sharp shake before lifting container straight up. If the plate has been rinsed in cold water first, the mold can be easily slid into a more accurate position. Refrigerate immediately. For large molds or multiple molds on a single platter, or when the mold is to be served on a bed of shredded lettuce, etc., the hot-water dipping method is not feasible. Containers should be inverted cold and warmed with hot damp towels, repeating until container lifts free.

AVOCADO MOLD

2 large ripe avocados
1/4 cup garlic olive oil*
1/4 cup lemon or lime juice
1 envelope gelatin
3 tablespoons water
1/4 teaspoon each salt, white pepper and
　　onion powder
1/4 cup mayonnaise
2 6-1/2-ounce cans broken shrimp,
　　rinsed and drained
1 cup heavy cream, whipped
parsley sprigs
tiny thin slices of lemon

*See glossary

Peel and dice avocado and marinate in oil and lemon or lime juice 2 hours. Soften gelatin in cold water and dissolve over hot water. Cool. In blender, purée avocado and juices, gelatin, seasonings, mayonnaise and shrimp. Fold in cream and adjust seasonings to taste. Pour into a 4- to 5-cup mold, cover and chill at least 6 hours.

Turn mold out onto serving platter and garnish with parsley and lemon slices. Serve with water crackers, melba rounds or other plain crackers.

Makes approximately 40 buffet servings

molds

BLUE CHEESE MOLD

1 envelope gelatin
3 tablespoons cold water
6 ounces Gorgonzola cheese
4 ounces cream cheese, softened
3/4 cup heavy cream
1/2 teaspoon onion powder
1/4 teaspoon white pepper
1 beaten egg white
20 pimiento-stuffed olives

Soften gelatin in cold water and dissolve over hot water. Mash cheeses and blend in cream, onion powder and gelatin. Add pepper and adjust to taste. Fold in egg white and pack into a 2- to 3-cup mold. Cover and chill at least 4 hours.

Turn mold out onto serving platter. Slice some of the olives and decorate top of mold. Finely mince remaining olives and arrange around mold. Serve with crackers, raw vegetables and/or buttered bread.

Makes approximately 30 buffet servings

CAVIAR MOLD

1 envelope gelatin
3 tablespoons cold water
2 eggs, separated
2 tablespoons heavy cream
4 ounces cream cheese, cut into bits
2 tablespoons lemon juice
1 tablespoon freshly grated lemon rind
1 teaspoon Worcestershire sauce
1 3-3/4-ounce jar lumpfish caviar
1/2 cup heavy cream, whipped

Presentation
1 3-3/4-ounce jar lumpfish caviar
  or
20 black olives, halved
2 hard-cooked eggs, whites and yolks
  sieved separately

Soften gelatin in cold water and dissolve over hot water. Cool. In large saucepan, beat yolks and cream. *Stirring constantly,* cook over medium low heat *just* to heat. Add cheese and stir until cheese melts. Remove from heat. Blend in lemon juice, rind, Worcestershire sauce and caviar. Whip egg whites until stiff and fold into whipped cream. Gently fold into caviar mixture. Pour into a 3- to 4-cup mold; cover and chill at least 6 hours.

Turn mold out onto serving plate. Decorate with caviar or black olives and hard-cooked eggs.

Makes approximately 40 buffet servings

BRAUNSCHWEIGER-CREAM CHEESE MOLD

12 ounces braunschweiger, softened
8 ounces cream cheese, softened
3 tablespoons finely minced green onions
1 tablespoon lemon juice
1-1/2 teaspoons Worcestershire sauce
6 drops Tabasco
1/4 teaspoon each salt, white pepper and
    garlic powder

Presentation
8 ounces cream cheese, softened
1 tablespoon half-and-half
1/2 cup chopped toasted almonds
10 small pimiento-stuffed olives, sliced

Combine ingredients and blend thoroughly. Adjust seasonings to taste. Chill.
Form pâté into desired shape and place on serving plate. Mix cheese and half-and-half until thin enough to spread. Coat pâté and decorate with almonds and olives. Serve with melba rounds, cocktail rye or plain crackers.
Makes approximately 60 buffet servings

HORSERADISH MOLD

1 envelope gelatin
1/2 cup cold water
1/2 cup hot water
1 tablespoon vinegar
1/2 cup prepared horseradish
1/8 teaspoon garlic powder
1/4 teaspoon salt
1 teaspoon sugar
1-1/2 cups sour cream

Soften gelatin in cold water and dissolve in hot water. Add remaining ingredients and stir until smooth. Pour into well-oiled 3- to 4-cup mold. Chill until firm and serve with cold baked ham, beef or corned beef. Attractive when surrounded with fresh parsley and cherry tomatoes.
Makes approximately 40 buffet servings

pates

CHICKEN LIVER PÂTÉ

1 pound chicken livers, cut up
dry sherry to cover
1 cup chopped onion
1 teaspoon minced garlic
3 tablespoons each butter and rendered
    chicken fat
1 teaspoon salt
1/4 teaspoon each white pepper, turmeric,
    paprika and nutmeg
3 tablespoons butter, softened
2 tablespoons dry sherry or brandy

Presentation
1 hard-cooked egg, yolk and white sieved separately
minced black olives
parsley sprigs
aspic cutouts (page 18)

Marinate livers in sherry 2 to 4 hours. Drain. Sauté
onion and garlic in butter and fat 3 minutes. Add
livers, sprinkle with seasonings and sauté, stirring
often for 10 minutes to stiffen livers and cook
partially. Purée in blender; add butter and sherry.
Blend. Correct seasonings and chill.
Mound pâté on serving plate and decorate with
eggs, olives, parsley and aspic cutouts. Mound
finely chopped aspic in one corner and serve with
melba rounds, cocktail rye, pumpernickel or plain
crackers.
Makes approximately 40 buffet servings

Variations
• Season with one of the following: dry mustard,
thyme, Worcestershire sauce, chili powder, paprika,
dill weed, lemon juice, ground cloves, ginger or
tarragon.

To the pâté add:
• Chicken gizzards cooked in water with bay leaf,
salt and pepper, then puréed with livers.
• Finely minced mushrooms sautéed with livers
(1/2 pound each).
• Shelled green pistachios or other nuts, chopped.
• Chopped ripe olives, ham, hard-cooked egg.
• Crisp bacon bits.

CHICKEN LIVER MOUSSE

1 envelope gelatin
3 tablespoons cold water
1-1/2 cups chicken liver pâté, preceding,
    room temperature
1 tablespoon brandy or to taste
3 tablespoons chopped black olives
1/2 cup heavy cream, whipped
black olive halves

Soften gelatin in cold water and dissolve over hot
water. Cool. Beat liver pâté and brandy until
smooth. Stir in softened gelatin and olives. Gently
fold in whipped cream. Garnish top with olives.
Makes approximately 2-1/2 cups

BAKED CHICKEN LIVER PÂTÉ

1 pound chicken livers, cut up
sherry to cover
2 tablespoons each butter and
    rendered chicken fat
1/2 cup minced onion
1-1/2 teaspoons minced fresh tarragon
1/2 teaspoon minced garlic
1/4 teaspoon salt
1/8 teaspoon white pepper
1/4 cup heavy cream

Presentation
chopped or sieved hard-cooked eggs
parsley sprigs or watercress

Marinate livers in sherry 2 to 4 hours. Drain and
sauté in butter and fat with the onion, tarragon
and garlic 3 to 4 minutes to barely cook. Livers
should be pink inside. Purée in blender with seasonings and cream. Adjust seasonings to taste and
pour into a well-buttered 4-cup, round-bottom
baking dish. Cover tightly with heavy foil and place
in pan. Fill pan with boiling water halfway up sides
of pâté dish. Bake in a 325° oven 1-1/4 to 1-1/2
hours until set. Remove foil, cool, cover and chill
thoroughly.
Turn pâté out onto serving plate and decorate with
eggs. Garnish with parsley or watercress. Serve with
melba rounds or crackers.
Makes approximately 40 buffet servings

SPICY BAKED CHICKEN LIVER PÂTÉ

1/2 pound chicken livers, cut up
sherry to cover
1 egg
1/2 cup diced onion
1 teaspoon minced garlic
2 tablespoons each flour and softened butter
1/2 cup heavy cream
1 teaspoon salt
1/4 teaspoon each white pepper and
    powdered ginger
1/8 teaspoon each cinnamon, nutmeg and
    powdered cloves
tiny piece of bay leaf, crumbled

Marinate livers in sherry 2 to 4 hours. Drain. Purée
in blender with remaining ingredients. Sauté a
small amount and adjust seasonings. Pour into a
well-buttered, round-bottom 3-cup baking dish.
Follow preceding directions for baking and pre-
senting.
Makes approximately 25 buffet servings

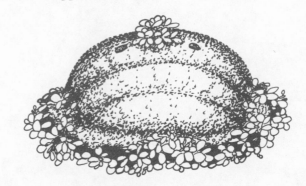

pates

TUNA PÂTÉ

6 ounces cream cheese, softened
1 7-ounce can oil-packed tuna fish
1 envelope gelatin
2 tablespoons brandy
1 4-ounce can chopped olives
2 hard-cooked eggs, chopped
1/4 teaspoon each salt and Tabasco
2 tablespoons minced parsley

Blend cream cheese and tuna in blender. Soften gelatin in brandy and dissolve over hot water. Add to blender with olives, eggs and seasonings. Blend until smooth and adjust seasonings to taste. Add parsley, pack into 2 crocks and refrigerate. Serve with crackers or toast.
Makes approximately 2-1/2 cups

PORK PÂTÉ

1 pound lean ground pork
1 cup coarsely grated onion
2 tablespoons heavy cream or evaporated milk
1/2 teaspoon each salt, savory and paprika
1/4 teaspoon black pepper
1/3 cup sour cream
2 teaspoons lemon juice

Presentation
1 hard-cooked egg, white and yolk
   sieved separately
1/4 cup minced chives or green onion tops
1 lemon, thinly sliced
parsley sprigs

Stirring often, cook pork, onion, cream and seasonings in double boiler 2 hours. Strain and purée in blender. Add sour cream and lemon juice. Blend to mix well and adjust seasonings. Pack into an oiled 3- to 4-cup mold, cover and chill at least 6 hours. Turn pâté out onto serving plate and decorate with eggs and chives or green onion tops. Arrange lemon slices and parsley around pâté. Serve with melba rounds, crackers or cocktail rye.
Makes approximately 30 servings

MOCK LIVER PÂTÉ

8 ounces braunschweiger
2 tablespoons each minced chives,
  parsley and green onion with tops
6 tablespoons butter, softened
2 tablespoons lemon juice, brandy or
  dry vermouth
1/2 teaspoon salt
1/4 teaspoon pepper

Presentation
1 recipe consommé jelly (page 17)
1/4 cup chopped pine nuts
8 strips canned pimiento
1/2 cup finely minced parsley
2 hard-cooked eggs, whites and yolks
  sieved separately

Combine ingredients and adjust seasonings. Chill. Form pâté into smooth oval on serving platter. Flatten top surface to make base for decorations. Prepare aspic and pour into large flat dish to fill about 1/4 inch. Chill to set and cut into shapes with hors d'oeuvre cutters. Arrange cutouts around edge of top surface of pâté and down the center make a band of pine nuts. Arrange pimiento in spoke fashion between aspic and nuts. Chop remaining aspic and mound in one corner of serving platter. Mound the parsley in another corner and put hard-cooked eggs along bottom edges of pâté. Serve with melba toast, water crackers or cocktail rye bread.
Makes approximately 50 buffet servings

RILLETTES

1 pound lean, tender cut of pork
1/4 cup rendered pork fat
3/4 pound fat back, thinly sliced and
  cut in small pieces
3 cups water
1-1/2 teaspoons salt
bouquet garni of:
  1 large bay leaf
  1/2 onion
  4 whole cloves
  4 sage leaves
  2 sprigs thyme
  1 sprig rosemary
  4 sprigs parsley
  8 peppercorns

Cut or shred pork into *tiny* pieces and pound in mortar and pestle. In heavy, large-bottom pan, brown pork well in rendered fat, stirring and scraping bottom of pan often. Pieces should be golden and crisp. Add fat back, water and salt and stir well to loosen meat from bottom of pan. Add bouquet garni, bring to gentle boil, cover and simmer slowly 5 hours. Stir occasionally and add more water if meat starts to dry. Fat will be melted in that time and pork will be very tender and will have absorbed the flavor of the herbs. Strain, discard bouquet garni and reserve fat. Pack into 2 2-cup crocks and over each pour 1/4 cup reserved fat. Cover and chill. Serve with lettuce and crusty French bread.
Makes 3-1/2 cups

pates

PÂTÉ EN CROÛTE

Pastry
3 cups flour
1/2 teaspoon salt
1/4 pound butter, cut into bits
4 tablespoons lard or shortening
3 egg yolks
1/2 cup or more ice water

Sift flour and salt and cut in butter and lard or shortening. Make a well in center and add egg yolks and water. Quickly blend with fork, adding more water if needed to make a smooth dough. Handle as little as possible. Form into a ball, wrap in wax paper and refrigerate at least 1 hour. If making a day ahead, place wrapped pastry in plastic bag.

Crêpes
2 eggs, beaten
1/2 cup flour
1/3 cup rich stock
vegetable oil

Combine eggs, flour and stock. Let stand 1 hour. Stirring often and adding more stock if too thick, pour about 1/4 cup into a heated and oiled heavy 9- or 10-inch skillet. Quickly tip skillet to coat bottom with batter. Cook until set, flip over and cook other side. Cool on rack and repeat, making 4 crêpes.

Forcemeat filling
1 pound each ground lean veal and pork
4 ounces beef kidney fat or fat back, ground
2 eggs, beaten
3 tablespoons fine bread crumbs
1/4 cup dry white wine
1-1/2 teaspoons salt
1/2 teaspoon pepper
1/4 teaspoon nutmeg

Blend ingredients thoroughly and sauté a small amount. Adjust seasonings to taste. Set aside.

To assemble
12 ounces cooked ham and/or tongue, cut into 1/4-inch square strips and marinated (see turkey galantine, page 82)
Madeira jelly (page 17)
watercress or parsley
black olives
lettuce cups

Butter sides and bottom of pâté en croûte or other mold. Roll pastry 1/8 inch thick and 1 inch larger than mold to be filled. Reserve remaining pastry for top and decorations. Place rolled pastry sheet in mold and press down against sides and bottom. Trim edges, leaving a 1/2-inch border. Moisten rim of mold and fold pastry over and under itself; press firmly against rim and bake in 450° oven 10 minutes. Cool. Line the bottom and sides of the mold with crêpes, reserving enough for top, and then add a 1/4-inch layer of forcemeat. Drain ham and/or tongue strips and lay 1/3 of them on the forcemeat. Cover with 1/3 of the remaining forcemeat and repeat twice more, ending with forcemeat. Top with reserved crêpes. Roll remaining pastry 1/2 inch larger than top of mold and place over filling and crêpes. Fold overlapping edge under itself to form a rim, press onto lower crust and crimp the resulting ridge. Make a small hole in the center of the covering and one near each end of mold. Hold open with small end of pastry tubes. Prick covering in several places with tines of fork and decorate with pastry cutouts. Brush with 1 egg beaten with 1 tablespoon water. Bake in 350° oven 45 minutes, cover top lightly with buttered brown paper and continue cooking 45 minutes longer. Remove from oven and cool 30 minutes. Pour jelly into holes, let run into pâté and repeat until pâté can hold no more jelly. Let stand in cool place 6 hours or until pâté is thoroughly cooled and jelly has set. Turn out on serving platter and garnish with watercress or parsley, olives and lettuce cups. Slice thinly. Makes approximately 20 slices

79

terrines

TERRINE OF PORK

1/2 pound pork liver, cut up
2 tablespoons butter
1/2 teaspoon sage
1/3 cup chopped onion
4 cloves garlic
1 pound each lean pork and veal
1/2 pound fat back
1/4 cup brandy
1-1/2 teaspoons salt
3/4 teaspoon allspice
1/2 teaspoon each pepper and mace
1 egg, beaten
fat back, very thinly sliced (enough to
    line terrine and cover top of pork mixture)
3 bay leaves or 6 tarragon leaves
fat back, melted

Sauté liver in butter, sprinkling with sage while cooking, until stiffened and almost cooked through. Cool. Using finest blade of grinder, grind liver, onion and garlic. Using coarsest blade, grind pork, veal and 1/2 pound fat back. Combine mixtures with brandy, seasonings and egg. Let stand 1 to 2 hours to blend flavors. Line a deep straight-sided 1-1/2- to 2-quart terrine dish with sliced fat back, pack meat mixture in and mound slightly. Lay bay leaves or tarragon on top, cover with fat back slices and then with foil. Place in a pan of hot water and bake in a 325° oven 1-1/2 to 2-1/2 hours, depending upon depth of terrine. Terrine is done when it pulls away from sides and liquid fat is clear. Remove from oven, discard foil, cool 10 minutes and place a piece of greased brown paper or wax paper on top, then a dish that fits inside. Weigh down, cool and refrigerate with weight. Remove from dish and scrape off fat. Wash dish and replace terrine. Pour melted fat back into dish to cover terrine. Serve from the terrine, or turn out on bed of shredded lettuce and slice. This may be frozen after baking. Good with French or other crusty bread.
Makes approximately 60 buffet servings

GALANTINES

Galantines can be true works of art, for not only do they lend themselves to creative surface decorating like canapes, but their internal structure can be designed so that new beauty is revealed as they're sliced. A real challenge to the artist-sculptor-cook, galantines are complex only in their lengthy preparation, not in the simple steps involved.

Their ancient origin is obscure, but undoubtedly related to the Latin verb *gelare*, to freeze, for they are dishes of rolled boned meat or fish filled with forcemeat and strips of meat, cooked in gelatin stock, wrapped, pressed and served cold, coated with an aspic of jellied stock. Chaucer knew them well, for he claimed never to be walled and wound in "galauntyne" as he was in love.

Five days should be allowed for preparation of galantines. Four days before serving day the ingredients should be purchased, the forcemeat ground, the meat boned and the ham or tongue cooked. The next morning the tongue, ham, uncooked fat back and boned meat trimmings are cut into strips or cubes and marinated with the boned meat 4 to 6 hours. Then the forcemeat is mixed and wrapped in boned meat with artistically arranged strips or cubes of tongue, ham, fat back and trimmings. The galantine is then wrapped in cloth, cooked and cooled in stock, weighed down and refrigerated. On the third day the cloth is removed, the galantine rewrapped in foil, and refrigerated that day and the next to mellow (or frozen up to 1 month). On serving day the foil is removed, the galantine is placed on a platter and multiple coatings of aspic or jellied stock are applied interspersed with decorative garnishes, with excess jelly on platter wiped away during the process. The galantine is now ready and should be kept covered and refrigerated until served. Aspic does not keep well so galantine should be served on the day of coating.

Galantines with their concentrated flavor are best served on slices of bread or with forks accompanied by bread chunks. They are excellent for a luncheon or supper buffet.

BONING FOWL

Lay fowl breast down and with small, sharp, thin, pointed knife, cut skin down backbone. With point always tight against bones, separate meat gradually down one side almost to the breastbone with short shallow strokes so as not to pierce the skin. Wing is removed at the shoulder and drumstick at the knee leaving minimum size holes in the skin. The hip joint is severed internally and the thigh bone removed with a single lengthwise slit on the inside and a gradual cutting away from the bone.

Repeat for other side. With almost-detached meat flat on either side and extra care to avoid slitting the skin, delicately cut away from breastbone leaving meat and skin intact and in one piece.

galantines

TURKEY GALANTINE

1 large turkey breast (approximately 6 pounds)
6 ounces cooked smoked tongue, cut into
   1/4-inch square strips
1/2 pound fat back, cut into 1/4-inch square strips

Marinade
1/2 cup brandy
3 parsley sprigs, separated
6 to 8 peppercorns, crushed
4 to 6 whole allspice, crushed

Stock
2-1/2 to 3 quarts water
bones from turkey breast
1 or 2 pounds veal knuckle and chicken bones
1 large pig's foot
1 carrot, sliced
1 onion stuck with 2 cloves
1 leek and some tops, chopped
parsley and thyme sprigs
6 peppercorns, crushed
2 teaspoons salt

Forcemeat
1 pound ground veal
1 egg
1/4 cup strained reserved marinade
1 teaspoon salt
1/4 teaspoon pepper
1/4 cup minced parsley

Glaze
1 envelope gelatin
3 tablespoons cold water
1/3 cup hot reserved stock
1/2 pint sour cream
garnishes/decorations (page 18)
1/4 cup or more coating jelly (page 17)

82

Debone turkey breast. Lay skin side down on board and with sharp knife trim ridges and fill valleys to make 3/4-inch even thickness. Place turkey breast and any excess trimmings in shallow glass baking dish with the tongue and fat back strips. Combine marinade ingredients and pour over. Cover and marinate, turning occasionally, 4 to 6 hours. Remove from marinade and set aside. Strain marinade and reserve.

Combine stock ingredients in large kettle, bring to gentle boil, skim off any scum that rises to top, cover and simmer 1-1/2 hours.

Combine forcemeat ingredients. Place turkey skin side down on board. Cover with half the forcemeat and arrange extra turkey pieces, tongue and fat back in alternate pattern on top. Cover with remaining forcemeat and starting from wide end roll turkey tightly, tying with string if necessary to keep roll even. Place on well-buttered square of muslin and tie with string. Tie ends like a sausage and lower into stock pot (if roll is very long use a roasting pan on 2 burners). Bring stock back to gentle boil, cover and simmer 2 hours, keeping at low boil. Tip lid slightly and cool in liquid. Remove galantine and place in shallow pan. Weigh down moderately with heavy pan or board and several plates. Galantine should be firm but all liquid should not be pressed out. Reheat stock, strain, clarify if necessary and jar. Cool, cover and refrigerate.

The next day, remove muslin from galantine, wrap well in foil and refrigerate. Several days of mellowing will improve flavor. Galantine may be frozen at this point.

To serve: Remove foil and place galantine on serving platter. Soften gelatin in water and dissolve in hot stock. Cool and blend in sour cream. Let stand 10 minutes or until starting to gel. Brush onto sides and top of galantine. Mixture should be firm enough to set at room temperature. Decorate and finish with a thin layer of coating jelly. Chill to set firmly, cover with saran wrap and refrigerate. Just before serving decorate platter with chopped aspic and other garnishes and surround with French or other crusty bread slices.

Makes approximately 30 to 40 buffet servings

galantines

CHICKEN GALANTINE

1 4- to 4-1/2-pound chicken
1/2 pound cooked ham, cut into
   1/4-inch square strips
1/2 pound fat back, cut into 1/4-inch square strips
2 to 3 tablespoons pistachio nuts

Marinade
see turkey galantine

Stock
see turkey galantine. Omit turkey bones and
   add bones from deboned chicken.

Forcemeat
2 chicken livers, halved
1 tablespoon butter
1/2 pound each ground pork and veal
1 egg
1/4 cup ground fat back
1/4 cup strained reserved marinade
1 teaspoon salt
1/4 teaspoon pepper

Glaze
1 cup coating jelly (page 17) with dry
   vermouth added, if desired
decorations/garnishes (page 18)

Bone chicken. Lay skin side down on board and with sharp knife trim ridges and fill valleys to make 3/4-inch thickness. Place boned chicken, any excess trimmings and trimmings from wings and legs, ham strips and fat back strips in shallow glass baking dish. Combine marinade ingredients and pour over. Cover and marinate, turning occasionally, 4 to 6 hours. Remove from marinade and set aside. Strain and reserve marinade.

Combine stock ingredients in large kettle, bring to gentle boil, skim off any scum that rises to top, cover and simmer 1-1/2 hours.

Sauté chicken livers in butter quickly to stiffen. Remove and chop. Combine with rest of forcemeat ingredients.

Lay chicken skin side down on board. Cover with half of the forcemeat, sprinkle with pistachio nuts, arrange extra chicken pieces, tongue and fat back in alternate pattern on top. Cover with remaining forcemeat and roll, cook in stock and refrigerate as directed for turkey galantine.

To serve: Remove foil and place galantine on serving platter. Cover with thick layer of coating jelly, decorate and finish with a thin layer of coating jelly. Chill to set firmly, cover with saran wrap and refrigerate. Just before serving decorate platter with chopped aspic and other garnishes and surround with crusty bread slices.

Makes approximately 25 buffet servings

VEAL GALANTINE

1 4-pound breast of veal (or 2 2-pound breasts)
1/2 pound cooked smoked tongue, cut
  into 1/4-inch square strips
1/2 pound fat back, cut into 1/4-inch square strips
2 to 3 tablespoons pistachio nuts

Marinade
see turkey galantine

Stock
see turkey galantine. Use the bones from the veal
breast and omit turkey bones.

Forcemeat
2 chicken livers, halved
1 tablespoon butter
1/2 pound each ground pork and veal
1 egg
1/4 cup minced parsley
1 teaspoon salt
1/4 teaspoon pepper
1/4 cup reserved strained marinade

Glaze
1 cup coating jelly (page 17) with dry
  vermouth added if desired
decorations/garnishes (page 18)

Debone breast of veal and place in shallow glass baking dish with the tongue and fat back. Combine marinade ingredients and pour over. Cover and marinate, turning occasionally, 4 to 6 hours. Remove and set aside. Strain and reserve marinade.

Combine stock ingredients in large kettle, bring to gentle boil, skim off any scum that rises to top, cover and simmer 1-1/2 hours.

Sauté chicken livers in butter quickly to stiffen. Remove and chop. Combine with rest of forcemeat ingredients.

Lay breast of veal flat on board (if using 2 overlap slightly). Cover with half of the forcemeat, sprinkle with pistachio nuts, arrange extra veal pieces, tongue and fat back in alternate patterns on top. Cover with remaining forcemeat and roll; cook in stock and refrigerate as directed in recipe for turkey galantine.

To serve: Remove foil and place galantine on serving platter. Cover with thick layer of coating jelly, decorate and finish with a thin layer of coating jelly. Chill to set firmly, cover with saran wrap and refrigerate. Just before serving decorate platter with chopped aspic and other garnishes and surround with crusty bread slices.

Makes approximately 25 buffet servings

soups and
stoppers

A stopper is a first course. It can be a soup ladled into attractive mugs or a mousse prepared in individual molds, served at the dining table for small groups or in the living room for larger groups. The choice of this first course must be made with specific considerations. It should be visually attractive, with special attention given to garnishes and serving equipment. Since several courses may follow the stopper, it should not be too filling. And of special importance, it must complement the other foods being served.

LETTUCE SOUP

9 cups shredded lettuce (1 large head)
3 cups rich chicken stock
3/4 cup chopped watercress
1 teaspoon sugar
1-1/2 cups half-and-half
3/4 teaspoon salt
1/2 teaspoon each garlic powder and white pepper
1/4 teaspoon nutmeg
1/3 cup butter, cut into bits
1/3 cup minced watercress for garnish

Combine lettuce, stock, watercress and sugar. Bring to gentle boil, cover and simmer until lettuce is soft. Purée a little at a time in blender. Return to saucepan, add half-and-half and seasonings; reheat and adjust to taste. Just before serving swirl in butter bits and garnish with watercress.
Serves 8 to 10

soups

SORREL SOUP

2 quarts lamb stock
1 cup rice, washed
1 cup half-and-half
1-1/2 cups finely chopped sorrel
1 tablespoon butter
1/2 teaspoon each oregano and thyme
1 teaspoon minced parsley
1/2 teaspoon salt
2 teaspoons lemon juice
finely minced lemon rind for garnish

Bring 2-1/2 cups stock to boil and add rice. Cover and simmer until rice is soft. Purée a little at a time in blender and force through sieve, pushing as much rice through as possible. Add half-and-half and rest of stock. Sauté sorrel in butter until it changes color. Add to soup with seasonings and lemon juice. Reheat and adjust. Fill mugs and sprinkle with lemon rind.
Serves 10 to 12

Variation
Use any good stock. Omit sorrel and mixed herbs and simply season to taste with curry powder, garlic powder, chili powder or herbs and spices of choice. Garnish each serving with a bit of grated sharp Cheddar cheese.

CLEAR TOMATO SOUP

1-1/2 cups diced onion
3/4 cup diced carrot
1/2 cup chopped celery
1 large clove garlic, minced
3 tablespoons butter
3 pounds ripe tomatoes, chopped
3 tablespoons tomato paste
1-1/2 teaspoons each sugar and salt
1/2 teaspoon white pepper
8 parsley sprigs
3 thyme sprigs
1 bay leaf
5 cups chicken stock

Garnish
minced parsley
or dollops of sour cream
or minced tarragon, dill, chives or mint
or thin slice of orange

Sauté onion, carrot, celery and garlic in butter, covered, until soft, adding more butter if needed. Add tomatoes, tomato paste, seasonings and herbs. Bring to gentle boil, cover and simmer 30 minutes. Discard thyme and bay leaf and strain, forcing as much pulp through sieve as possible. Add stock, cover and simmer 15 minutes. Adjust seasonings and garnish as desired.
Serves 8 to 10

SUNCHOKE SOUP

1 pound sunchokes (Jerusalem artichokes)
2 quarts boiling water
2 teaspoons salt
salt and white pepper
Chinese parsley*

*See glossary

Scrub sunchokes thoroughly. Drop into boiling salted water, cover and cook at gentle boil 15 minutes or until just tender-crisp. Drain and reserve liquid. When cool enough to handle, peel sunchokes and finely mince enough for 1 cup. Set aside. Reserve remaining sunchokes and use as suggested below. Heat cooking liquid and adjust with salt and white pepper. Add minced sunchokes, heat and ladle into mugs. Garnish each with small bits of Chinese parsley.
Serves 8 to 10

Variation
Melt 3 tablespoons butter until bubbly, stir in 3 tablespoons flour and cook and stir 3 minutes. Gradually add liquid and cook until slightly thickened. If desired, add dry white wine to taste.

Suggested uses for sunchokes
• Slice, heat with butter and sprinkle with minced parsley.
• Substitute for celeriac in celeriac salad filling (page 150).
• See sunchoke salad (page 149).

CUCUMBER SOUP

4 cups chopped, peeled and seeded cucumbers
1 cup chopped onion
1 clove garlic, minced
4 tablespoons butter
2 cups rich chicken stock
2 cups diced potato
1-1/2 cups half-and-half
1/2 cup heavy cream
1/2 teaspoon salt
1/4 teaspoon white pepper

Garnish
1/4 cup finely minced, peeled and
    seeded cucumber
2 tablespoons minced parsley

Sauté cucumbers, onion and garlic in butter until onion is soft. Add chicken stock and potato, bring to gentle boil, cover and cook until potatoes are soft. Purée in blender, add half-and-half, cream and seasonings. Reheat and adjust to taste. Garnish with minced cucumber and parsley.
Serves 8 to 10

soups

PEA SOUP

3 10-1/2-ounce packages frozen peas
6 cups rich chicken stock
2 whole cloves
1 bay leaf
6 parsley sprigs
3 green onions and tops, cut up
1 clove garlic, halved
1/2 teaspoon salt
1/4 teaspoon pepper
2 cups half-and-half
minced chervil or mint for garnish

Combine peas, 2 cups of the stock, cloves, bay leaf, parsley, onion, garlic, salt and pepper. Simmer until peas are tender, remove cloves and bay leaf and purée in blender. If smoother soup is desired, sieve. Add half-and-half and rest of stock. Reheat and adjust seasonings to taste. Fill mugs and sprinkle with chervil or mint. May be served chilled.
Serves 8 to 10

CHILLED HERB SOUP

4 cups chicken stock**
4 cups chopped watercress
2 cucumbers, peeled, seeded and chopped
1/2 cup chopped green pepper
1/4 cup each chopped onion, chives and sorrel
1/2 pint sour cream
1-1/2 teaspoons each salt and sugar
2 to 3 teaspoons lemon juice
sieved hard-cooked egg and paprika for garnish

In blender purée 1 cup of stock with half the vegetables, herbs and sour cream. Repeat with another cup of stock and the rest of vegetables, herbs and sour cream. Transfer to large bowl, add remaining stock and salt, sugar and lemon juice; adjust to taste. Chill at least 4 hours. When ready to serve, fill mugs and sprinkle with a little egg and paprika.
Serves 8 to 10

**If stock is very gelatinous, substitute water and chicken stock base for part of stock.

CHEESE-BEER SOUP

1/4 pound butter
1 medium-sized onion, finely chopped
1/2 cup flour
1 quart beer
4 cups grated Swiss cheese (or Swiss
    mixed with Monterey Jack)
2 quarts milk
parsley sprigs

Melt butter in a deep saucepan and add onion. Cook several minutes but do not brown. Add flour and cook until mixture bubbles, stirring constantly. Gradually add beer, stirring until smooth and thick. Add cheese to melt. Gradually add milk; heat but do not boil. Pour into mugs and garnish with a sprig of fresh parsley.
Serves 10 to 12

APPLE BUTTER SOUP

2 10-1/2-ounce cans consommé
1 cup water
1-1/2 cups heavy cream
1/2 to 1 teaspoon curry powder
1/3 cup apple butter
2 teaspoons lemon juice or to taste
1/3 cup sour cream

Combine consommé, water, cream, curry powder and apple butter. Heat and adjust to taste. *Just* before serving add lemon juice and float small dollops of sour cream on top.
This soup does not reheat well. Serve immediately after adding lemon juice.
Serves 4 to 6

stoppers

SEAFOOD COCKTAIL

1-1/2 pounds flaked crab meat, small cooked
   shrimp and/or lobster, cut up
2 tablespoons lemon juice
1 cup chili sauce
1/2 cup dry white wine
1 tablespoon lemon juice
2 tablespoons grated onion
1 to 2 teaspoons prepared horseradish
1 teaspoon dill weed
1/8 teaspoon garlic powder

Presentation
finely shredded lettuce
2 hard-cooked eggs, whites and yolks
   sieved separately
16 pitted black olives, cut into 4 strips

Toss seafood with lemon juice, cover and refrigerate 2 hours. Combine remaining ingredients, adjust to taste and chill.
Place lettuce in 16 small scallop shells or oyster shells. Arrange seafood on lettuce and top with sauce. Garnish with egg and olive strips.
Serves 16

POACHED EGGS IN ASPIC

2 cups water
1 teaspoon white vinegar
1/2 teaspoon salt
12 small eggs
consommé or tomato jelly (page 17)

Presentation
broken chicory or shredded iceberg lettuce
12 slices peeled tomato
homemade mayonnaise or remoulade sauce
minced chives
lemon wedges or curls

Bring water, vinegar and salt to boil and keep at gentle boil. Break 1 egg at a time into a dish, make a whirlpool in the water and slide egg into center. Cook gently until whites are set; with slotted spoon remove to large pan of ice water. Repeat with rest of eggs. Drain, trim edges and dry. Using small individual molds and tarragon leaf decoration, mold in aspic. Chill until set.
Place chicory on 12 plates, top with tomato slice and unmold egg on top. Pour a small amount of mayonnaise or remoulade sauce over, sprinkle with chives and garnish with lemon wedges or curls.
Serves 12

STUFFED TOMATOES

For 8 medium tomatoes
6 eggs, beaten
2 tablespoons half-and-half
3 tablespoons minced parsley
2 tablespoons minced chives
1/2 teaspoon salt
1/4 teaspoon pepper
2 tablespoons butter
1 recipe tomato sauce (page 10)
1/2 cup minced ham

Basic preparation for stuffed tomatoes: Dip in boiling water 1 minute or until skin comes off easily. Peel and cut small slice from top. Hollow out and turn upside down to drain, reserving pulp for soup or other use. Sprinkle tomato shells with salt and pepper before filling.
Beat eggs, half-and-half, parsley, chives and seasonings. Melt butter and cook egg mixture until set but not dry, stirring occasionally. Combine with tomato sauce and ham and fill tomatoes.
Serves 8

Variations
• Mix reserved pulp with curried egg salad, fill and top with small cooked shrimp, crab leg and/or parsley or watercress sprigs and tiny lemon peel.
• Stuff with cooked marinated green beans, pour 1 teaspoon French dressing over and garnish with sliced hearts of palm.

CHICKEN MOUSSE

1 envelope gelatin
3 tablespoons dry white wine
1-1/4 cups hot rich chicken stock
1-1/2 cups chopped chicken (or 1 cup
    chicken and 1/2 cup chopped ham)
1 tablespoon brandy
1/2 teaspoon salt (less if using ham)
1/4 teaspoon each white pepper and paprika
1/8 teaspoon nutmeg
1/2 cup heavy cream, whipped
1/4 cup finely chopped blanched almonds
    (optional)

Presentation
12 small Bibb or butter lettuce cups
homemade mayonnaise
finely chopped aspic
parsley sprigs

Soften gelatin in wine and dissolve in stock. Purée in blender with chicken and ham. Add brandy, seasonings and adjust to taste. Chill, stirring occasionally, until almost set. Fold in cream and optional almonds. Brush individual molds with oil and fill with mousse mixture. Chill until firm.
Unmold mousse on lettuce on individual plates. Top with dab of mayonnaise and garnish with mound of aspic and parsley sprig.
Serves 12

stoppers

CHEESE CUSTARD MOLDS

2 cups milk, scalded and cooled
4 eggs, beaten
6 tablespoons finely grated Gruyère cheese
1/2 teaspoon salt
1/4 teaspoon white pepper
1/8 teaspoon nutmeg
1/4 cup ground ham or cooked shrimp

Presentation
finely shredded daikon*
tomato sauce (page 10)
parsley

*See glossary

Combine ingredients and fill 8 1/2-cup or slightly larger molds which have been well buttered and then coated with bread crumbs. Place in pan of hot water and bake in a 350° oven 10 minutes or until toothpick inserted in center comes out clean. Cool. Turn molds out onto daikon on individual plates. Pour a little tomato sauce over each and garnish with parsley.
Serves 8

TOMATO CUSTARD MOLDS

3 pounds tomatoes
3 tablespoons butter
1-1/2 teaspoons sugar
3/4 teaspoon salt
1/2 teaspoon each pepper and basil
5 eggs, beaten

Presentation
watercress
bay or canned shrimp or crab legs

Cook tomatoes, butter and seasonings until tomatoes are very soft. Sieve and cook down to 2-1/2 cups. Cool, adjust seasonings and beat in eggs. Pour into 10 1/2-cup molds which have been well buttered and then coated with fine bread crumbs. Put molds in pan of hot water and bake in 350° oven 10 minutes or until toothpick inserted in center comes out clean. Cool.
Turn molds out onto bed of watercress on individual plates. Garnish with shrimp or crab.
Serves 10

SNAIL CANAPE

12 small rounds of bread (1-1/2 inches in diameter)
12 medium-sized fresh mushrooms
12 canned French snails
1/4 pound butter, softened
1 clove garlic, minced
bread crumbs
finely chopped parsley

Toast bread rounds. Wash mushrooms and remove stems. Blanch mushroom caps in hot water and drain on paper toweling. Place a mushroom on each bread round. Fit a snail into each mushroom cap. Combine butter and garlic and cover each snail with about 1/2 teaspoon of mixture. Sprinkle with bread crumbs. When ready to serve, arrange canapes on baking sheet and heat in a 350° oven for 8 to 10 minutes. Remove from oven, sprinkle with parsley and serve hot.
Makes 12

Variation
With hands, mold bite-sized meatballs from any of the appetizer meatball recipes. Substitute for snails in the cap of the mushroom. Bake as directed for snail canapes.

PRAWNS STUFFED WITH CLAMS

2 pounds large prawns, shelled and deveined
1-1/4 cups bread crumbs
1/2 teaspoon each salt, paprika and garlic powder
1/4 teaspoon each pepper and thyme
1/4 cup minced parsley
1/3 cup softened butter
2 7-1/2-ounce cans minced clams, drained
dry sherry
lemon slice twists

Split prawns lengthwise halfway through. Combine crumbs, seasonings and parsley; work in butter and add clams. Stuff slit in prawns with clam mixture. Place 2 prawns in each of 12 to 14 small buttered scallop shells or oyster shells. Drizzle a little sherry over and bake in 350° oven 15 minutes, basting several times with more sherry. Raise heat to 425° to brown. Serve immediately with lemon.
Serves 12 to 14

stoppers

SPINACH PIE

1 10-1/2-ounce package frozen chopped spinach
2 eggs, beaten
2 tablespoons finely minced onion
3 tablespoons grated Romano or Parmesan cheese
1/2 teaspoon salt
1/4 teaspoon each pepper and garlic powder
1/8 teaspoon nutmeg
1-1/2 tablespoons butter

Defrost spinach, press out all moisture and finely chop. Combine with eggs, onion, cheese and seasonings. Heat butter until bubbly and add spinach mixture. With spatula pat into large circle about 1/2 inch thick. Cook over medium heat until browned. Under medium broiler brown top of pie. Eggs should be set and pie should be cooked through. Transfer to serving plate, cool and chill. To serve cut in wedges.
Makes 16 to 20 servings

LOBSTER-MUSHROOM COQUILLES

1/2 pound mushrooms, minced
3 tablespoons butter
1/4 cup minced shallots
3 tablespoons flour
1-1/2 cups half-and-half
1/2 teaspoon each salt, dry mustard and paprika
1/4 teaspoon each garlic powder, white
    pepper and celery salt
2 egg yolks
1/4 cup dry sherry
2 teaspoons lemon juice
1/2 teaspoon curry powder
2-1/2 cups chopped cooked lobster meat
3 tablespoons minced parsley

Presentation
12 to 14 small buttered scallop or oyster shells
buttered bread crumbs
grated Parmesan cheese
parsley sprigs
lemon curls

Sauté mushrooms in butter until slightly browned. Add shallots and cook 2 minutes. Sprinkle with flour, stir and cook 3 minutes. Slowly add half-and-half. Cook and stir until thickened. Add seasonings. Beat yolks and sherry and whisk in 1 cup hot mushroom sauce. Beat into rest of sauce and add lemon juice and curry powder. Cook and stir without boiling 5 minutes. Adjust seasonings and add lobster and parsley. Cool and refrigerate to blend flavors.

Divide lobster mixture between shells and sprinkle with crumbs and cheese. Bake in 350° oven 15 minutes or until bubbly and browned. Garnish each plate with parsley and lemon curls.

Serves 12 to 14

stoppers

EGGPLANT ROLLS

1 large, long, slender eggplant, peeled if desired
flour
1/4 cup olive oil
2 tablespoons butter
Parmesan cheese and chopped parsley for garnish

Filling
1 cup grated Mozzarella cheese
1/2 cup grated Parmesan cheese
1/2 cup small curd cottage cheese
1 egg
1 tablespoon each finely chopped
    parsley and prosciutto
1/8 teaspoon salt
1/16 teaspoon white pepper
1 egg white, stiffly beaten

Batter
2 tablespoons flour
1/2 teaspoon baking powder
1/8 teaspoon salt
1 egg
1/3 cup milk
1 tablespoon salad oil

Sauce
1 cup tomato sauce
1/2 teaspoon oregano
1 tablespoon white dry vermouth

Filling: In a bowl combine cheeses, egg, parsley, prosciutto, salt and pepper. Mix well. Fold in stiffly beaten egg white. Set aside.

Batter: In a separate bowl sift together flour, baking powder and salt. Add egg, milk and salad oil. Beat until smooth. Set aside.

Sauce: Combine tomato sauce, oregano and vermouth in a small bowl and stir until well blended. Set aside.

Cut stem end from eggplant. Slice eggplant in half lengthwise. Beginning from cut surface, cut each half into 6 lengthwise slices, as thin as possible and no more than 1/16th of an inch thick. Dredge slices lightly in flour then dip into prepared batter. Heat olive oil and butter in a large skillet and fry slices until slightly browned on each side. Remove and drain on paper toweling. Continue this procedure until all slices have been cooked.

To assemble: With wide side of eggplant slice toward you place 2 tablespoons of the prepared cheese filling about 1 inch from the edge of the slice. Roll, jelly roll fashion. Place roll, seam side down into a shallow, lightly buttered baking dish. Continue, until all slices have been filled. (If made ahead, stop at this point, cover dish with plastic wrap and refrigerate.) Spoon prepared sauce over eggplant rolls and bake in a 375° oven 25 to 30 minutes or until heated through. If dish has been refrigerated add 10 minutes to baking time. This is an ideal first course when served in individual dishes and topped with a sprinkle of Parmesan cheese and chopped parsley.
Serves 12

SHRIMP SAUCE ON TOAST

3 tablespoons each butter and flour
1-1/2 cups dry white wine
1/2 cup heavy cream
1/2 pound Emmenthaler or Gruyère cheese, diced
3 tablespoons minced parsley
2 tablespoons minced chives
1/2 teaspoon salt
1/4 teaspoon each white pepper and paprika
3 eggs, beaten
1-1/2 cups cooked shrimp, cut up

Presentation
6 pieces white bread, crusts removed
buttered bread crumbs
paprika
parsley sprigs

Melt butter until bubbly, sprinkle with flour and cook and stir 3 minutes. Gradually add wine and cream. Cook and stir until smooth and thickened. Add cheese, parsley, chives and seasonings. Stirring constantly, cook to melt cheese. Beat eggs with 1/2 cup of hot cheese sauce and beat into rest of sauce. Add shrimp, cook and stir 5 minutes. Do not boil. Toast bread and cut each piece into 4 triangles. Place 2 in each of 12 buttered scallop shells or small ramekins. Pour sauce in, top with bread crumbs, sprinkle with paprika and broil until bubbly. Garnish with parsley.
Serves 12

STOPPER SUGGESTIONS

• Marinate Crenshaw or cantaloupe balls in sherry to cover 1 hour or coat avocado balls with lemon juice. Place in bottom of chilled bowls and spoon finely chopped aspic over. Top with 1 to 2 tablespoons caviar and sprinkle with chopped chives and sieved hard-cooked egg yolk.
• Wrap lemon-coated avocado balls or melon balls in prosciutto.
• Combine cantaloupe balls with anchovies.
• Place crab, shrimp or lobster in small scallop shells or oyster shells; dress with homemade mayonnaise seasoned with sieved hard-cooked eggs, minced pickle or pickle relish, brandy and paprika.
• Place halved oysters on bed of ice. Serve with lemon wedges and buttered thinly sliced pumpernickel.
• Place marinated mushrooms in lettuce cups. Sprinkle with paprika and minced parsley.
• Serve grapefruit sections with chutney.

pastries

phyllo/quiches/tarts

PASTRIES

The secret of light pastry is to handle as little as possible. After mixing, always form dough into a ball, wrap in wax paper and refrigerate at least 1 hour. A long, thin Italian rolling pin is the easiest to use for rolling. Work with a small portion of the pastry at a time, keeping unused pastry wrapped and chilled. Place on lightly floured board (Wondra flour works well) and press down with heel of hand. With spatula, lift and turn over. Lightly flouring board and rolling pin, roll gently from center out; repeat until 1/4 to 1/16 inch thick, depending upon recipe. Cut and fill as directed, place on ungreased cookie sheet and continue with rest of pastry. Incorporate scraps in next amount used. Toward the end when pastry has started to dry out, it may be necessary to use a little water to seal edges.

• *Freezing:* Pastries freeze well and can be stored up to 3 months. For fillings that do not freeze see page 20.

• *Baking:* Chill, covered, 30 minutes. Brush with egg wash (beat 1 egg with 1 tablespoon water) if desired and bake in 375° oven 15 to 30 minutes depending upon size. Since oven temperatures vary, watch carefully.

• *Leftovers:* Leftover fillings can be used in many ways: mix with scrambled eggs, fill toast cups, use in phyllo triangles or rolls. Pastry scraps may be rolled, spread with softened butter and sprinkled with cinnamon-sugar, sesame seeds or grated cheese and baked.

COTTAGE CHEESE PASTRY

Sift 1-1/4 cups unbleached flour with 1/2 teaspoon salt and 1/4 teaspoon mace (optional). Cut in 1/4 pound butter until crumbly. With fork, stir in 1/2 cup creamed small curd cottage cheese and 2 tablespoons milk.

CREAM CHEESE PASTRY

Sift 1 cup plus 2 tablespoons unbleached flour with 3/4 teaspoon salt and 1/4 teaspoon mace (optional). Cut in 1/4 pound each butter and cream cheese until crumbly. With fork, blend in 1 beaten egg.

CHEDDAR CHEESE PASTRY

Sift 1-1/4 cups unbleached flour, 1/2 teaspoon salt and 1/8 teaspoon cayenne pepper or 1/4 teaspoon nutmeg or mace. Combine 1/4 pound butter and 2 cups grated Cheddar cheese and work into flour mixture.

QUICK CHEESE PASTRY

Sift 2/3 cup flour and 1/8 teaspoon cayenne pepper. Cut in 1/4 pound butter and blend in 1 5-ounce jar processed cheese.

Variations:
Add 2 tablespoons onion soup mix, or 1/4 teaspoon nutmeg, or 2 tablespoons sesame seeds.

pastries

SOUR CREAM PASTRY

Sift 1-1/2 cups unbleached flour, 1 teaspoon salt and 1/4 teaspoon mace (optional). Cut in 1/4 cup cold butter which has been cut into small bits until mixture has coarse lumps. With fork, stir in 5 to 6 tablespoons sour cream to make pastry just moist enough to form into ball.

SHORT CRUST PASTRY

In mixer beat 1 cup lard or shortening until smooth and creamy. Beat in 1/3 cup boiling water and 1 tablespoon milk until liquid is blended into shortening. With fork stir in 2-1/2 cups unbleached flour sifted with 1 teaspoon salt.

Variations
• Sift 1/2 teaspoon Italian seasoning or 1/8 teaspoon garlic powder or 1/4 teaspoon mace or other herb when sifting flour.
• Add ground ham and/or finely minced parsley to shortening before adding flour.
• Substitute 1 tablespoon lemon juice for milk if using for salad shell.

QUICK PUFF PASTRY

Puff pastry consists of paper-thin layers of dough separated by paper-thin layers of butter or shortening. During baking, the dough layers puff and the pastry rises. The butter eases the separation of the layers. Steam is caught between the layers of dough forcing them to rise, and as baking continues, the steam evaporates and the fat is absorbed leaving a tender, flaky pastry. Puff pastry can also be purchased frozen or in bulk from some bakeries. Cut 1/4 pound butter into 20 pieces, place in a bowl and chill 20 minutes. With fingers, briefly and quickly work in 1 cup minus 2 tablespoons cake flour to blend only slightly. With fork stir in 1/4 cup ice water. Turn out onto board floured with 2 tablespoons cake flour. Roll 1/4 inch thick, fold into thirds and roll again. Repeat several times until butter is incorporated. Use as little flour as possible. After rolling: when cutting, cut with quick pressure from top; do not draw knife or pastry wheel through pastry or it will tear.
If using frozen patty shells, thaw in refrigerator overnight. On a floured board or pastry cloth, stack and press together 2 pastry shells. Roll into a rectangle, turn dough over and trim to 5x9 inches or form into desired shape. Bake as directed for puff pastry. (Leftover scraps may be chilled, rolled, cut into any shape and sprinkled with seasoned salt, cheese or poppy seeds. Prick with a fork before baking in a 400° oven 8 to 10 minutes.)

PIZZA DOUGH

1 tablespoon dry yeast
1/4 cup lukewarm water
1/2 cup milk
1/2 teaspoon salt
2 tablespoons shortening
1-1/2 cups flour

Dissolve yeast in water. Combine milk, salt and shortening. Heat to dissolve shortening. Cool to lukewarm. Combine with yeast and gradually add flour. Turn out on floured board and knead 10 minutes or longer until smooth and elastic. Place in greased bowl and grease top lightly. Cover with tea towel and let rise in warm place 1-1/2 hours or until double in bulk. Punch down and on floured board pat and roll 1/4 inch thick. Cut into 5 5-1/2-inch circles and bring edges up to make a rim. May be frozen at this point. Or form into 2-inch circles for buffet pizzas. Recipe may be doubled.
Makes 5 5-inch pizzas or 40 2-inch pizzas

BOUCHÉES

1 recipe quick puff pastry (page 102)

Working with half the pastry at a time (follow general directions for working with pastry) roll pastry 1/8 inch thick. Cut into 1-1/2-inch rounds and place half the rounds on cookie sheet. With a 1-inch cutter cut centers from second half of rounds. Place a ring on each round. Chill and repeat with rest of pastry. Chill 30 minutes before baking. Bake in 400° oven 10 minutes or until golden. With small fork scrape a little of the puffed center out to make a shell. May be frozen before baking. Defrost 1 hour in refrigerator. Never fill until just before serving. Note: If pastry is not rolled out evenly, the shells will tend to tilt while baking. Resulting taste is still the same but appearance is not!

Fillings
• Sour cream seasoned to taste with lemon juice, then topped with red or lumpfish caviar.
• Any of the choux fillings, hot or cold.

pastries

DIRECTIONS FOR MAKING PASTRY ROLLS

Divide specified pastry into 4 parts, roll each 1/8 inch thick into a rectangle about 9x12 inches. Cut in half lengthwise and spread with 1/8th of the filling, leaving a 1/4-inch border. Roll tightly like jelly roll, seal and place seam side down on cookie sheet. Bake at 375° 15 to 20 minutes or until golden.

PORK PASTRY ROLLS

1 double recipe cream cheese pastry (page 101)
1 pound lean ground pork
1/2 cup crab meat or chopped cooked shrimp
1/2 teaspoon salt
1/2 cup minced water chestnuts
1/4 cup finely minced bamboo shoots
2 tablespoons minced green onions and tops
2 teaspoons finely minced ginger root
1 teaspoon minced garlic
2 tablespoons soy sauce
1 egg, beaten
1/4 cup bread crumbs
1/2 teaspoon sesame oil*

*See glossary

Cook pork until it loses color; do not brown. Add crab or shrimp and rest of ingredients. Break off a small portion and cook to test for seasonings. Add more bread crumbs if mixture is runny. Follow preceding directions for making rolls. After baking let cool 3 or 4 minutes before cutting into 1-inch diagonal slices.

Makes approximately 120

PUFF PASTRY SQUARES

Prepare 1 recipe quick puff pastry (page 102). Roll dough 1/8 inch thick, cut into 1-1/2-inch squares. Place 1/2 teaspoon filling on square, top with another and press gently to seal. Brush with an egg mixed with 1 teaspoon water. Bake at 375° for 15 to 20 minutes or until golden.
Makes approximately 3 dozen

• *Gorgonzola Filling* Combine 1 cup crumbled Gorgonzola cheese (6 ounces), 1 egg yolk, 1 teaspoon Worcestershire sauce, 3 tablespoons minced green onions and tops, 2 tablespoons minced parsley and 3 drops Tabasco. Adjust to taste with salt and white pepper if needed.
• *Ham Filling* Combine 1 cup finely minced ham, 2 tablespoons grated onion, 2 tablespoons minced parsley, 2 tablespoons finely minced sweet pickles and Dijon-style mustard to taste. Adjust with salt and pepper if needed.
• *Gruyère Cheese Filling* Combine 1 beaten egg, 1 beaten egg yolk, 1 tablespoon melted butter, 1/3 cup grated Gruyère cheese, salt and cayenne pepper. After filling and brushing with egg wash, sprinkle with more grated cheese.
• *Anchovy Filling* Mash anchovies with sweet butter, lemon juice, pepper and Dijon-style mustard.

• *Seafood Filling* Over low heat blend 2 tablespoons flour into 2 tablespoons melted butter. Add 1 cup milk and stir until thickened. Season with sherry and grated cheese and add finely minced cooked shrimp or crab. Add salt, white pepper and cayenne pepper to taste.
• *Other Filling Ideas* Liver pâté, or grated Cheddar cheese and caraway seeds, or butter seasoned with anchovy paste and minced green onions.

PUFF PASTRY FINGERS

1 recipe puff pastry (page 102)
1 egg, beaten with
1 tablespoon water
1/2 cup finely grated Cheddar, Monterey
   Jack or Gruyère cheese
paprika
cayenne pepper

Roll pastry 1/4 inch thick. Brush with egg beaten with water. Sprinkle with cheese, paprika and light dusting of cayenne. Cut into 1/2-inch strips 2 inches long. Twist into spiral and place on lightly buttered or oiled baking sheet. Bake in 375° oven 10 to 15 minutes until puffed and golden. Serve immediately.
Makes approximately 6 dozen

pastries

SAUSAGES WRAPPED IN PASTRY

1 recipe cream cheese pastry (page 101), or
  puff pastry (page 102)
2-1/2 pounds link pork sausages

Place sausages on a rack in a baking pan and bake
in 350° oven 30 minutes or until slightly browned.
Drain on paper toweling and cut into halves or
thirds depending upon size of sausages. Roll pastry
1/8 inch thick and cut into 1-1/4-inch squares.
Place sausage piece on corner of square and roll to
partially wrap. Place seam side down on cookie
sheet. Chill 1 hour, or freeze up to 2 months. Bake
in 375° oven 15 minutes or until pastry is golden.
Makes approximately 5 dozen

PASTRY BALLS

Roll short crust pastry (page 102), cream cheese
pastry (page 101) or Cheddar cheese pastry (page
101) 1/4 inch thick. Cut into 1-1/2-inch rounds.
Form around any suggestions below and bake in a
375° oven 15 minutes or until golden. Cool slightly
before serving. May be frozen before baking.
• Tiny steak tartare balls.
• Small cubes of cooked veal.
• Small cubes of cheese.

DIRECTIONS FOR MAKING PASTIES

Roll specified dough 1/16 inch thick, cut into
1-1/2-inch rounds or 1-1/4-inch squares. Place 1/2
teaspoon filling on round or square, top with
another and press gently to seal. Bake at 375° for
15 to 20 minutes or until golden.

CHEESE PASTIES

1 double recipe short crust pastry (page 102)
1 egg, beaten
1 cup crumbled Gorgonzola cheese (6 ounces)
1 cup shredded Gruyère cheese
1/4 pound butter, softened
1/3 cup minced green onions and tops
3 tablespoons minced parsley
1/2 teaspoon Worcestershire sauce or to taste
4 drops Tabasco

Divide beaten egg in 2 bowls. Blending in thoroughly, to one bowl add the Gorgonzola and half
remaining ingredients. To the other add the
Gruyère and remaining ingredients. Follow preceding directions for making pasties.
Makes approximately 12 dozen

MUSHROOM PASTIES

1 recipe short crust pastry (page 102)
3/4 pound mushrooms
1 cup water
1 teaspoon lemon juice
1/4 teaspoon salt
4 tablespoons butter
1/2 cup finely minced green onions and tops
3 tablespoons minced parsley
2 tablespoons minced shallots (optional)
1 teaspoon finely minced garlic
1/2 teaspoon each salt and paprika
1 tablespoon lemon juice
1/4 teaspoon Tabasco
2 tablespoons flour
1/2 cup sour cream

Remove stems from mushrooms, mince caps and set aside. Simmer stems in water, lemon juice and salt, uncovered, 30 minutes. Drain and discard stems; reserve liquid. Melt butter and sauté onion, parsley, shallots, garlic and minced caps 5 minutes. Season with salt, paprika, lemon juice and Tabasco; sprinkle with flour, cook and stir 3 minutes. Gradually add 1/2 cup reserved mushroom liquid; cook and stir until thickened. Blend in sour cream and cook without boiling 2 minutes. Adjust seasonings and cool. Follow preceding directions for making pasties.
Makes approximately 6 dozen

SHRIMP PASTIES

1 recipe cream cheese pastry (page 101)
1-1/4 cup minced cooked shrimp
1/4 cup each minced green onions and tops and minced water chestnuts
1 teaspoon Dijon-style mustard
1/4 cup mayonnaise
1 teaspoon Worcestershire sauce
1/4 teaspoon each salt, pepper and basil
2 teaspoons lemon juice

Combine ingredients and adjust seasonings to taste. Follow preceding directions for making pasties.
Makes approximately 4 dozen

pastries

CHOUX

1 cup water
1/4 pound butter
1/2 teaspoon salt
1/8 teaspoon each nutmeg and white pepper
1 cup unbleached flour
5 eggs
fillings of choice

Heat water, butter and seasonings until butter is melted. Bring to rolling boil, add flour all at once and remove from heat. Stir with wooden spoon until batter is smooth and leaves the side of saucepan. Cool 2 minutes. Beat in 4 of the eggs, one at a time, blending well after each addition. Let rest 15 minutes or cover and refrigerate up to 4 days. On greased cookie sheets, form tiny mounds with a spoon or pastry tube about 1 inch in diameter and 1/2 inch tall. Lightly brush tops with 1 egg beaten with 1 teaspoon water and bake in 400° oven 10 minutes. Reduce heat to 325° and bake 15 minutes more or until golden. Remove from oven and quickly prick an edge of each chou with tines of fork to let air out. Shut off oven heat and return choux to oven for 5 minutes with door open. Remove from cookie sheets and cool on racks. Slit tops and fill. If hot fillings are used reheat in a 350° oven. *Do not fill with cold fillings until shortly before serving.* If freezing, make a heavy foil "box" for desired number to freeze. Seal well and freeze up to 1 month. To bake, open foil a bit to expose choux, defrost and heat in a 400° oven 15 minutes. Makes approximately 80

Variations
• Use clam juice or milk in place of half the water. Season with 1/4 teaspoon each dill weed and thyme and 1 teaspoon minced chives.
• Add 1/3 cup grated Gruyère cheese after adding the eggs.
• For dessert add 1 teaspoon each sugar and rose water or orange water to batter.

Fillings for Hot Choux
• Melt 2 tablespoons butter until bubbly; sprinkle with 2 tablespoons flour. Cook and stir 3 minutes and gradually add 1-1/3 cups half-and-half. Cook and stir until smooth and thickened. Add 3/4 cup ground ham, 3 sieved hard-cooked eggs, 1 tablespoon each finely minced green pepper and pimiento and salt and white pepper to taste. Add 1/4 cup grated cheese if desired.
• Make preceding cream sauce and add 1-1/2 cups chopped cooked shrimp and 2 tablespoons dry sherry. Add nutmeg, salt and white pepper to taste.
• Combine 6 ounces cream cheese, 1-1/2 cups flaked crab meat or chopped cooked shrimp, lemon juice, Worcestershire sauce, dill weed, Tabasco, salt and pepper to taste. Add 1/4 cup grated cheese if desired.
• Drain 3 7-1/2-ounce cans minced clams and combine with 6 ounces cream cheese and 2 tablespoons minced chives. Add seasoned salt, pepper and Tabasco to taste.
• Drain and flake 1 7-ounce can tuna and combine with 1 cup finely minced zucchini and 1/3 cup mayonnaise. Add lemon juice, salt, pepper and paprika to taste.
• Combine 1-1/2 cups minced cooked chicken breasts with 3 tablespoons finely minced celery. Add lemon juice, curry, salt and pepper to taste, and mayonnaise to bind.
• Mushroom or tomato-ham duxelle (page 12).
• Cream cheese softened with heavy cream and seasoned to taste with curry powder, mustard, paprika, salt and pepper.

Fillings for Cold Choux
• Combine 1 cup ground ham and 3 to 4 tablespoons finely chopped walnuts. Bind with chili sauce and season to taste with Tabasco.
• Mash 1 avocado with 2 teaspoons lemon juice and blend in 1/4 cup sour cream. Season to taste with grated onion, finely minced peeled and seeded tomatoes, salt, pepper and Tabasco.
• Season sour cream or softened cream cheese with grated onion and white pepper to taste. Fill puff and top with lumpfish caviar and lemon peel.
• Combine 1 cup minced cooked lobster, crab or shrimp with 1/2 cup mayonnaise. Add dry mustard, minced capers, minced gherkins, tarragon, salt and pepper to taste.
• Chicken, salmon or tuna salad.
• Combine 6 ounces cream cheese, 2 or 3 mashed sardine fillets and 3 tablespoons each minced parsley and chives. Add lime or lemon juice, salt and pepper to taste.
• Chop cucumbers finely, sprinkle with salt, let stand 30 minutes, rinse, drain and squeeze in cheesecloth. Bind with mayonnaise and season to taste with grated onion, minced parsley, salt and pepper.
• Finely grate celery root and mix with drained minced capers, minced chives, salt and pepper to taste. Bind with mayonnaise.
• Combine 1/2 cup cooked minced mushrooms, 1 cup minced cooked chicken and 1/4 cup coarsely chopped blanched almonds. Add nutmeg, salt and white pepper to taste.

pastries

DIRECTIONS FOR MAKING PIROSHKI AND EMPANADITAS

Roll specified dough 1/16 inch thick, cut into 2-1/4-inch rounds, fill with 3/4 teaspoon filling, fold over to make half-moon shape and press gently to seal. Place seam side up for piroshkis; lay empanaditas on their sides. Bake at 375° for 15 to 20 minutes or until golden.

CHILI EMPANADITAS

1 recipe cream cheese pastry (page 101)
1 cup grated sharp Cheddar cheese
2 tablespoons softened butter
2 to 4 tablespoons canned Jalapeño green
   chilies, seeded and finely minced
1/4 cup each minced ripe olives and green
   onions and tops
1/2 teaspoon oregano
1/4 teaspoon each salt and pepper

Combine ingredients and adjust to taste. Be careful with the chilies; strength varies. Follow preceding directions for making empanaditas.
Makes approximately 4 dozen

BEEF EMPANADITAS

1 recipe cream cheese pastry (page 101)
3/4 pound lean ground beef
1/4 cup water
1/4 cup minced onion
1 teaspoon minced garlic
1/2 teaspoon each salt and oregano
1/4 teaspoon each pepper, thyme,
   cumin and chili powder
1 tablespoon tomato paste
6 drops Tabasco
1/2 to 1 teaspoon Worcestershire sauce
1 tomato, peeled and chopped
3 tablespoons grated Parmesan cheese
1/3 cup grated sharp Cheddar cheese

Brown meat and add water, onion, garlic, seasonings, tomato paste, Tabasco, Worcestershire sauce and tomato. Blend and simmer 30 minutes until moisture has evaporated. Cool and add cheeses. Adjust to taste. Follow preceding directions for making empanaditas.
Makes approximately 4 dozen

BEEF PIROSHKI

1 recipe cottage cheese pastry (page 101)
1 pound lean ground beef
2 tablespoons beef stock
1 tablespoon flour
3/4 cup minced onion
2 tablespoons butter
1 tablespoon minced fresh dill weed
1/2 teaspoon salt
1/4 teaspoon each pepper and paprika
3 hard-cooked eggs, chopped

Simmer beef and stock until meat loses color; do not brown. Sprinkle with flour; cook and stir 3 minutes. Set aside. Sauté onion in butter until soft, add to meat with seasonings and with fork gently stir in eggs. Adjust seasonings. Follow preceding directions for making piroshki.

Makes approximately 4 dozen

CHICKEN PIROSHKI

1 recipe cottage cheese pastry (page 101)
3/4 cup finely minced mushrooms
1/2 cup minced onion
3 tablespoons butter
1-1/2 cups finely minced cooked chicken
1 cup cooked rice
1/2 teaspoon salt
1/4 teaspoon each white pepper, paprika
    and savory
3 hard-cooked eggs, chopped

Sauté mushrooms and onion in butter until soft. Add chicken and cook rapidly until slightly browned. Mix in rice and seasonings. With fork mix in eggs. Adjust seasonings. Follow preceding directions for making piroshki.

Makes approximately 4 dozen

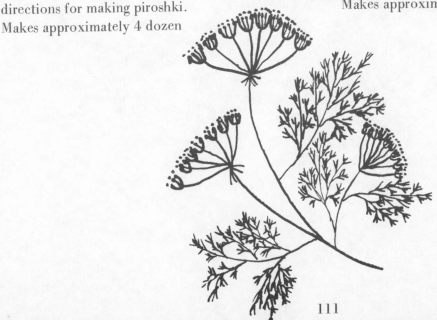

phyllo

PHYLLO

Phyllo dough is almost identical to strudel dough and is very difficult to make. It may be purchased in 1-pound packages in Greek and Armenian specialty shops and in many delicatessens. If frozen, always defrost overnight in the refrigerator. Well wrapped it will keep up to a week.

The sheets, 20 to 24 in a package, dry out rapidly and are easily broken. Take out 4 sheets at a time, reroll and rewrap the rest and cover with a slightly dampened cloth. (If dough gets wet it will be ruined.) With a feather brush, paint brush or other soft brush, spread one layer at a time with melted butter, stacking as you work. If sheets break, they can be "mended" with another sheet. Work quickly.

Note: Filled phyllo freezes well and can be kept up to 3 months if well-wrapped. Make different fillings for variety. For fillings that do not freeze see page 20.

PHYLLO TRIANGLES

Cut the 4 buttered layers widthwise into 10 even strips. Place 1-1/2 teaspoons of filling on the bottom of each strip. Fold over and continue in flag fashion, straight edge up, cross over, up cross over to make triangle. Be careful no filling shows at tips of triangle. Tuck last fold under, sealing with melted butter. Place seam side down 2 inches apart on ungreased cookie sheet and brush with melted butter. Never use so much butter that dough becomes soggy. To bake: Bake in a 375° oven 15 minutes or until golden. Watch carefully. Cool slightly before serving as filling stays very hot!

PHYLLO ROLLS
(Cigars)

Working with 2 sheets at a time, cut buttered sheets widthwise into 5 even strips. Place 1-1/2 teaspoons filling on end 1/2 inch from sides. Roll, tucking in sides. Seal with melted butter and place seam side down 2 inches apart on ungreased cookie sheet. Bake in a 375° oven 15 minutes or until golden.

CHICKEN-CHEESE FILLING FOR PHYLLO

1/4 cup minced onion
1/4 pound mushrooms, minced
2 tablespoons butter
2 cups finely minced cooked chicken
2 tablespoons minced parsley
1/2 teaspoon minced fresh tarragon or basil
1/2 teaspoon salt
1/4 teaspoon white pepper
1 egg, beaten
3/4 cup shredded Gruyère or
    Emmenthaler cheese

Sauté onion and mushrooms in butter until soft. Combine with rest of ingredients and adjust seasonings. Follow directions for making phyllo triangles or rolls.
Makes 50 to 60

SPINACH FILLING FOR PHYLLO

1/2 cup minced onion
2 tablespoons butter
1 10-ounce package frozen, chopped spinach, defrosted and *well* drained
1/2 cup minced parsley
2 tablespoons each minced fresh dill weed and minced chives
1/4 pound feta cheese, crumbled
2 eggs, beaten

Sauté onion in butter until soft. Combine with remaining ingredients and follow directions for making phyllo triangles.
Makes 50 to 60

phyllo

CRAB FILLING FOR PHYLLO

1/2 cup finely minced onion
2 ounces mushrooms, finely minced
3 tablespoons butter
2 tablespoons flour
3/4 cup chicken stock
1/2 cup minced parsley
1 tablespoon minced canned pimiento
2 teaspoons dill weed
1/2 teaspoon Worcestershire sauce
1/4 teaspoon white pepper
3 drops Tabasco
1/2 pound crab, finely flaked
2 teaspoons lemon juice

Sauté onion and mushrooms in butter, covered, over low heat until soft. Sprinkle with flour; cook and stir 3 minutes. Gradually add stock; cook and stir until thickened. Add remaining ingredients. Adjust seasonings to taste, adding salt if needed, and set aside to cool. Follow directions for making phyllo triangles or rolls.
Makes 50 to 60

FETA CHEESE FILLING FOR PHYLLO
(Tiropetes)

6 ounces feta cheese, crumbled
2 ounces cream cheese, softened
1 egg, beaten
1/4 cup minced green onion
1 tablespoon minced parsley
1 teaspoon each minced chives and dill weed

Combine ingredients and test for salt and pepper. Follow directions for making phyllo triangles or rolls.
Makes 50 to 60

Variation #1
1/2 pound feta cheese, crumbled
1/2 cup minced parsley
1 egg, beaten
1/2 teaspoon each cumin, oregano and thyme
1/4 teaspoon pepper
1/8 teaspoon cayenne pepper
Combine and adjust seasonings.

Variation #2
6 ounces each feta cheese, crumbled, and
    Monterey Jack cheese, shredded
1 egg, beaten
1/2 cup minced parsley
2 tablespoons minced green onions and tops
salt and pepper to taste
Combine ingredients.

VEAL FILLING FOR PHYLLO

3/4 pound ground veal
3 tablespoons minced onion
3 tablespoons butter
2 tablespoons each tomato paste and
  dry vermouth
1/2 teaspoon salt
1/4 teaspoon white pepper
1/8 teaspoon nutmeg
1/3 cup crumbled feta cheese
1 egg, beaten
2 to 3 teaspoons fine bread crumbs
2 tablespoons minced parsley

Brown veal and onion in butter. Add tomato paste, vermouth and seasonings. Cook until dry but still spreadable. Cool. Add remaining ingredients and adjust seasonings. Follow directions for making phyllo triangles or rolls.
Makes 50 to 60

Variation Use 1/2 pound veal and 2 tablespoons each minced onion and butter. Omit feta cheese and bread crumbs and add 3 ounces Gorgonzola cheese and 6 ounces cream cheese. Proceed as directed above.

BÖREKS
(Also Bureks, Berag)

3/4 pound ground lean beef (or
  half beef and half pork)
3 tablespoons minced onion
1 teaspoon minced garlic
1/4 cup pine nuts (optional)
2 tablespoons butter
1/2 teaspoon salt
1/4 teaspoon pepper
1/4 cup each tomato paste and dry red wine
4 ounces feta cheese, crumbled
1 egg, beaten
3 tablespoons minced fresh coriander*
1 package phyllo

*See glossary

Brown beef, onion, garlic and pine nuts in butter. Season and stir in tomato paste and wine. Cook and stir until thick. Cool. Add cheese, egg and coriander. Adjust seasonings. If too runny thicken with *fine* bread crumbs. Follow directions for making phyllo rolls. Serve on wooden plate with sliced cooked sausages, salami, green peppers and olives.
Makes 50 to 60

quiches

PREBAKED QUICHE SHELLS

1 recipe short crust pastry (page 102), or
  puff pastry (page 102)

Use a flan ring on a buttered cookie sheet, butter a spring-form, straight-sided pan or special flan pan with removable bottom, or, if planning to serve directly from pan, an ordinary pie plate. Roll pastry 1/8 to 1/4 inch thick in a circle 1-1/2 inches larger than pan. Gently place in pan and work pastry down inside edges. Trim, fold the overhang and flute edges, forming a slight ridge around top rim. Chill 30 minutes. Line with wax paper, fill with beans or rice and bake on middle rack of oven at 400° 10 minutes. Remove beans or rice and reserve for another time. Discard wax paper and lightly prick bottom of shell. Bake 4 more minutes. Remove from oven and cool. Refrigerate or wrap well and freeze. Sprinkle with 1 to 2 teaspoons Wondra flour, fill as directed in individual recipes and bake in a 375° oven 25 to 30 minutes for 8- or 9-inch quiche, 30 to 40 for 10-inch. Quiche is done when toothpick inserted in center comes out clean. Cool 3 minutes before cutting into wedges; serve immediately or at room temperature. Never reheat nor freeze after filling. To remove from pan, lift flan ring off (or set spring-form pan on jar and lift off ring) and with spatula carefully slide onto rack.

An 8-inch shell holds about 2-1/2 cups filling and serves 6 for supper or brunch, 16 to 20 for buffet; a 9-inch shell holds about 3 cups and serves 8 for supper or brunch, 20 to 24 for buffet; a 10-inch shell holds about 3-3/4 cups and serves 10 to 12 for supper or brunch and about 30 for buffet. For large groups: Use 10x15-inch jelly roll pans. To serve, cut into small squares.

CHEESE QUICHE

1 8-inch prebaked pastry shell
1 cup minced onion
2 tablespoons butter
1 cup half-and-half
2 eggs, beaten
1/2 teaspoon salt
1/4 teaspoon pepper
2 cups grated Gruyère cheese
1/2 teaspoon paprika

Sauté onion in butter until soft and slightly browned. Cool and place in shell. Beat half-and-half, eggs, salt and pepper. Sieve mixture and add cheese. Pour over onions, sprinkle with paprika and bake according to preceding directions.

Variations: Add 1/4 cup cooked crisp crumbled bacon or minced ham and minced parsley.

GREEN TOMATO QUICHE

1 8-inch prebaked pastry shell
1/2 cup finely minced onion
1/2 teaspoon finely minced garlic
1 tablespoon butter
3 to 4 green tomatoes, thinly sliced
1/2 teaspoon salt
1/4 teaspoon each pepper, oregano and sugar
1/4 cup grated Cheddar cheese
3 tablespoons minced parsley
2/3 cup grated Gruyère cheese
1 cup half-and-half
2 eggs, beaten
1/2 teaspoon paprika

Sauté onion and garlic in butter until soft; cool. Sprinkle tomatoes with seasonings and combine the Cheddar cheese and parsley. Sprinkle shell with half the Gruyère cheese and arrange half the seasoned tomatoes on top. Sprinkle with Cheddar cheese and parsley and top with remaining tomatoes. Beat half-and-half and eggs and sieve over filling. Sprinkle with remaining Gruyère cheese and paprika. Bake according to preceding directions.

ASPARAGUS QUICHE

1 8-inch prebaked pastry shell
1/2 to 3/4 pound asparagus
1/4 cup minced green onion, whites only
1 tablespoon butter
1 cup half-and-half
2 eggs, beaten
1/2 teaspoon salt
1/4 teaspoon each white pepper and savory
1/2 cup grated Gruyère cheese
paprika

Slice asparagus on diagonal, parboil 3 to 5 minutes and drain. Sauté onion in butter until soft and combine with asparagus. Arrange in pastry shell. Beat half-and-half, eggs and seasonings. Sieve over asparagus and sprinkle with cheese and paprika. Bake according to preceding directions.

quiches

SPINACH QUICHE

1 8-inch prebaked pastry shell
1 10-1/2-ounce package frozen chopped spinach
3 tablespoons finely minced shallots
1/2 teaspoon finely minced garlic
2 tablespoons butter
3/4 cup half-and-half
2 eggs, beaten
1/2 teaspoon salt
1/4 teaspoon each pepper and nutmeg
1/2 cup grated Gruyère cheese
1/2 teaspoon paprika

Cook spinach, drain thoroughly and reserve 1/4 cup liquid. Set aside. Measure 1 cup of the spinach and chop finely. Sauté shallots and garlic in butter until soft. Beat half-and-half and eggs, seasonings and reserved spinach liquid. Sieve and mix in spinach, shallots and garlic. Pour into shell and sprinkle with cheese and paprika. Bake as directed.

Variations: Add drained minced clams, or minced bay shrimp, or finely flaked crab meat, or crumbled cooked bacon. Reduce salt to 1/4 teaspoon.

MUSHROOM QUICHE

1 10-inch prebaked pastry shell
3 tablespoons minced shallots
1/2 teaspoon minced garlic
3 tablespoons butter
1 pound mushrooms, thinly sliced
1/2 teaspoon each salt and oregano
1 teaspoon lemon juice
1/4 cup minced parsley
1-1/4 cups grated Gruyère cheese
1-1/2 cups half-and-half
3 eggs, beaten
1/4 teaspoon pepper
1/8 teaspoon each cayenne pepper and sugar
1/2 teaspoon paprika

Sauté shallots and garlic in butter 3 minutes; add mushrooms and sprinkle with salt, oregano and lemon juice. Stir and cook until moisture is evaporated. Blend in parsley and cool. Place in pastry shell and sprinkle with 1/2 cup of the cheese. Beat half-and-half, eggs, peppers and sugar and sieve over mushrooms. Sprinkle with remaining cheese and paprika. Bake according to preceding directions for quiches.

ZUCCHINI QUICHE

1 9-inch prebaked pastry shell
2 zucchini (about 1 pound)
salt
2 tomatoes, peeled and quartered
1/2 cup finely minced onion
1/2 teaspoon finely minced garlic
1 tablespoon butter
1/2 teaspoon each salt and oregano
1/4 teaspoon pepper
1/2 cup grated Parmesan cheese
1 cup grated Gruyère or Tybo cheese
1 cup half-and-half
2 eggs, beaten
1/8 teaspoon cayenne pepper
1/2 cup grated Cheddar cheese

Thinly slice zucchini and sprinkle with salt. Place on paper toweling and let stand about 1 hour to draw out moisture. Pat dry. Squeeze out seeds from tomatoes and drain well. Sauté onion and garlic in butter until soft; cool. Combine seasonings and Parmesan cheese. Line shell with Gruyère cheese and cover with half the zucchini, tomatoes and seasoned Parmesan. Repeat. Beat half-and-half, eggs and cayenne and sieve over filling. Sprinkle with Cheddar cheese and bake according to preceding directions.

CRAB QUICHE

1 10-inch prebaked pastry shell
1/2 cup minced whites of green onions
1/4 cup finely minced celery
2 tablespoons minced shallots
1/2 teaspoon minced garlic
2 tablespoons butter
2-1/2 cups flaked crab meat
2 tablespoons minced parsley
1-1/2 cups half-and-half
3 eggs, beaten
1/4 teaspoon each salt, nutmeg and white pepper
1/8 teaspoon cayenne pepper
1 cup grated Gruyère or Emmenthaler cheese
1/2 teaspoon paprika

Sauté onions, celery, shallots and garlic in butter until soft. Cool. With fork stir in crab and parsley. Place in pastry shell. Beat half-and-half, eggs and seasonings. Sieve over crab and sprinkle with cheese and paprika. Bake according to preceding directions.

tarts

SMALL TARTS

1 recipe sour cream or short crust or
  Cheddar or quick cheese pastry (pages 101, 102)
choice of following fillings

Roll pastry 1/8 inch thick. Cut into 2-1/2-inch
rounds, prick entire surface with tines of fork and
lower gently into tiny muffin tins, shaping to fit
pan. Brush with slightly beaten egg white and bake
10 to 12 minutes in 375° oven. Remove and cool
on rack. Do not fill until just before serving. If
slightly larger tart is preferred, cut into 3- to
3-1/2-inch rounds, prick entire surface and form
around the outside of tiny muffin tins, pressing
gently to fit.
Makes 24 small tarts

• *Egg Filling* Combine 6 hard-cooked eggs, 6 tablespoons mayonnaise, 1/4 teaspoon each seasoned
salt and salt, 1 teaspoon prepared mustard, 1/8
teaspoon dill weed, 3 or 4 drops Tabasco and 2
tablespoons finely chopped pimiento (optional).
• *Shrimp Filling* Combine 1/4 pound chopped
small bay or canned shrimp, 1/2 cup mayonnaise,
1/4 cup finely diced green onion, 1/4 teaspoon
seasoned salt and 1 tablespoon minced parsley.
• *Olive-Nut Filling* Combine 1 cup chopped black
olives, 1/2 cup finely chopped walnuts, 1/2 cup
mayonnaise, 1/8 teaspoon onion salt and 1/4 cup
finely chopped celery (optional).

CROUSTADES

Keeping pastry as cold as possible, roll puff pastry
(page 102) 1/8 to 1/4 inch thick. Cut into 4-1/2-
inch rounds, line 6 lightly buttered 5-ounce custard
cups and crimp edges. Prick sides and bottom and
line with wax paper. Fill with beans or rice and
place in 450° oven. Immediately reduce heat to
425° and bake 12 minutes. Remove beans or rice
and discard paper. If using for hot croustades, bake
3 minutes longer, remove from cup, cool on rack,
fill and bake as directed for quiches. If using for
cold croustades, bake 10 minutes longer or until
golden, remove from cups and cool on rack. Fill
with one of the suggested cold choux or any other
cold fillings just before serving.
• *Peanut Butter Filling* Combine 1/2 cup peanut
butter (with or without chopped peanuts), 1/4 cup
finely chopped celery, 1/2 cup chopped seedless
raisins and 1/4 cup mayonnaise. Place mixture into
a large pastry bag fitted with a decorating point
large enough to allow the mixture to flow easily.
• *Ham Filling* Combine 3/4 cup ground cooked
ham, 3 tablespoons minced parsley, 2 tablespoons
catsup, 1 teaspoon Dijon-style mustard, 1/2 teaspoon Worcestershire sauce, brandy, salt and white
pepper to taste.
• *Cheese Filling* Combine 3 ounces each Gorgonzola and cream cheese, 1 tablespoon butter,
brandy, salt and pepper to taste.

chafing dish cookery

chafing dish

DEEP-FRIED SHRIMP BALLS

1 pound raw shrimp, shelled and deveined
1/3 cup finely minced water chestnuts
2 tablespoons minced green onions
1/2 teaspoon each finely minced garlic and
    ginger root
1 egg, beaten
1 tablespoon cornstarch
1 tablespoon each sherry and soy sauce
vegetable oil for frying

For Dipping
mustard
soy sauce
catsup

Mince shrimp very finely and combine with rest of ingredients. Chill. Form into balls approximately 1-1/4 inches in diameter. Fry in deep hot oil until golden. Drain on paper toweling and keep hot in chafing dish. Serve with cocktail picks and a dip of mixed mustard, soy sauce and catsup to taste.
Makes 40 to 50 balls

ABALONE BALLS

2 slices bacon
1 16-ounce can abalone pieces, well drained
1-1/4 cups graham cracker pieces
3/4 cup minced onion
2 tablespoons chopped olives
1 teaspoon dry mustard
1/4 cup minced parsley
2 eggs, beaten
2 tablespoons lemon juice
1/2 teaspoon each salt, thyme and paprika
1/4 teaspoon white pepper
3 to 4 tablespoons butter

Presentation
mustard
catsup
tartare sauce
whiskey sauce (page 8)

Cook bacon until crisp. Drain and reserve drippings. Grind bacon, abalone, graham crackers, onion and olives. Mix in mustard, parsley, eggs, lemon juice, seasonings and bacon drippings. Adjust seasonings to taste. Chill. Form into 1-inch balls and chill at least 1 hour. Sauté in butter to brown all sides. Transfer to chafing dish and serve with side dishes of mustard, catsup, tartare sauce and/or whiskey sauce.
Makes 3 dozen balls

PORK-CLAM BALLS

2 7-1/2-ounce cans minced clams
1 pound mild pork sausage
1 egg, beaten
2 tablespoons each fine bread crumbs and
 reserved clam liquid
1 tablespoon minced parsley
1/4 teaspoon each sage and pepper

Drain clams and reserve liquid. Combine with rest of ingredients, adding salt if needed. Chill. Form into 1-inch balls and chill 1 hour. Bake in a shallow baking pan in a 400° oven 7 minutes. Turn and bake 7 minutes more. Transfer to chafing dish and pour following sauce over balls.
Makes 4 dozen

Sauce for Pork-Clam Balls
3 tablespoons each butter and flour
1/2 cup reserved clam liquid
1-1/3 cups half-and-half or milk
1 tablespoon fresh minced dill weed
1 to 2 tablespoons dry sherry
salt and white pepper

Melt butter until bubbly, sprinkle with flour, cook and stir 3 minutes. Gradually add clam liquid and half-and-half; cook and stir until smooth and thickened. Add dill and just before serving blend in sherry. Adjust to taste with salt and white pepper.

POLPOTTE

1/2 pound each ground veal and lean beef
1 tablespoon each minced Italian parsley*
 and fresh grated lemon peel
1 teaspoon finely minced garlic
1/2 teaspoon salt
1/4 teaspoon each black pepper and oregano
2 tablespoons fine bread crumbs
1 egg, beaten
beef broth

*See glossary

Combine ingredients except beef broth and chill 1 hour. Form into 1-inch balls and place on shallow baking sheet. Do not crowd. Bake in a 375° oven 10 minutes, turning once, or until just cooked through. Transfer to chafing dish. To juices in pan add enough beef broth to moisten meatballs while keeping hot. Serve with cocktail picks.
Makes 4 dozen balls

Variations
Add 1 cup finely chopped spinach, blanched 1 minute and well drained and/or 1/2 teaspoon chopped fresh basil or finely minced onions and/or mushrooms.

chafing dish

SAUERKRAUT BALLS

2/3 cup minced onion
2 tablespoons butter
2 cups each flour and milk
1/4 cup minced parsley
1 teaspoon each dry mustard and salt
1-1/2 pounds ground cooked ham, canned beef
  or pork, or combination
1 1-pound, 11-ounce can sauerkraut,
  drained and finely chopped
2 to 3 beaten eggs
1-1/2 cups fine bread crumbs

Sauté onion in butter until soft. Stir in flour, milk, parsley, mustard and salt. Cook and stir 5 minutes. Mixture will be very thick and gummy. Cool. Combine ground meat and sauerkraut and add to flour mixture. Mix thoroughly and adjust seasonings. Chill. Form into 1-1/4-inch balls, dip in egg and roll in bread crumbs. Refrigerate or freeze. Fry in oil or shortening until golden and drain on paper toweling. May be made ahead and reheated in 350° oven.
Makes approximately 12 dozen

CHICKEN/TURKEY BALLS IN WINE SAUCE

1 pound ground chicken or turkey
1 egg, beaten
3 tablespoons each finely minced bamboo shoots,
  water chestnuts, green onions and tops,
  celery, parsley and bean sprouts (optional)
3 to 4 tablespoons fine bread crumbs
1/2 teaspoon each nutmeg or ginger,
  paprika and salt
1 teaspoon finely minced garlic
2 teaspoons lemon juice
2 to 4 tablespoons butter

Wine Sauce
3/4 cup dry white wine
1/2 pint sour cream
2 teaspoons each soy sauce and lemon juice

Combine all ingredients except butter. Sauté a small amount and adjust seasonings to taste. Chill. Form into 1-inch balls and refrigerate 1 hour. Turning often, sauté in butter 7 minutes or until cooked through. Remove to chafing dish.
Deglaze pan with wine, bring to boil and cook rapidly to reduce by half. Gradually add sour cream and season with soy sauce and lemon juice. Adjust to taste and pour over chicken balls. Serve with cocktail picks.
Makes 4-1/2 to 5 dozen balls

SWEET-SOUR MEATBALLS

Meatballs
2 pounds lean ground beef or ground turkey
1 egg, beaten
1 large onion, grated
1 teaspoon finely minced garlic
1 teaspoon salt
1/2 teaspoon black pepper
2 tablespoons water
1/4 cup fine bread crumbs
1 8-ounce can water chestnuts

Sauce
1 12-ounce bottle chili sauce
1 10-ounce jar grape jelly
2 teaspoons lemon juice
1 teaspoon Lemon Luau*

Presentation
1 8-ounce can pineapple chunks
1 6-ounce jar pimiento-stuffed olives

*See glossary

Combine meatball ingredients except water chestnuts. Cut water chestnuts into thirds or fourths and form meat around each to make a ball 1-1/4 inches in diameter. Chill.

Simmer sauce ingredients until thoroughly blended. Adjust to taste. Add meatballs and simmer 15 to 20 minutes until just done, stirring occasionally to keep from sticking. Transfer to chafing dish and add pineapple chunks and pimiento-stuffed olives. Serve with cocktail picks.

Makes 9 to 10 dozen buffet servings

chafing dish

LAMB MEATBALLS
(Two Variations)

1 cup finely minced onions
2 teaspoons finely minced garlic
2 tablespoons butter
2 pounds lean ground lamb
2 eggs, beaten
1/4 cup each fine bread crumbs and minced parsley
2 teaspoons salt
1/2 teaspoon black pepper

1/8 teaspoon each celery salt, powdered ginger,
    cardamom and curry powder

1/4 cup chopped olives
1 teaspoon freshly grated lemon peel
1/4 teaspoon allspice

Suggested Dips
yoghurt sauce (page 11)
sour cream and caraway seeds to taste
aioli sauce (page 6)

Sauté onions and garlic in butter, covered, until soft. Do not brown. Combine with lamb, eggs, bread crumbs, parsley, salt and pepper. Divide into 2 portions. To one add the celery salt, ginger, cardamom and curry. To second portion add olives, lemon peel and allspice. Test for seasonings and adjust. Chill 1 hour and form into 1-inch balls. Place in shallow baking dish (do not crowd) and bake in a 400° oven 15 minutes, turning once. Serve in chafing dishes with cocktail picks and dip of choice.
Makes 8 to 9 dozen

MINTED LAMB MEATBALLS

1 pound ground lean lamb
1 egg, beaten
2 tablespoons each fine bread crumbs,
    chopped fresh mint and minced parsley
3 tablespoons minced green onions and tops
1/2 cup chopped blanched spinach,
    well drained (optional)
1 teaspoon salt
1/4 to 1/2 teaspoon cumin
1/4 teaspoon black pepper

Combine ingredients and adjust for seasonings. Chill 1 hour and form into 1-inch balls. Place in shallow baking pan (do not crowd) and bake in a 400° oven 15 minutes, turning once. Transfer to chafing dish and serve with cocktail picks and one of dips suggested for lamb meatballs.
Makes 4 to 4-1/2 dozen

CREAMED SWEETBREADS

2 pounds cooked sweetbreads, see following
1/2 pound mushrooms, sliced
1/3 cup butter
1/2 cup flour
2 cups each half-and-half and liquid from
    cooking sweetbreads
1-1/2 cups diced ham
1 teaspoon salt
1/2 teaspoon each white pepper and thyme
1/4 cup each lemon juice and dry sherry
toasted slivered blanched almonds or
    drained capers (optional)
paprika
minced parsley and chives

Cook sweetbreads according to recipe, reserving cooking liquid. Sauté mushrooms in butter until just brown, sprinkle with flour, cook and stir 3 minutes. Slowly add half-and-half and sweetbreads cooking liquid. Cook and stir until thickened. Add cooked sweetbreads, ham and seasonings. Transfer to chafing dish and add lemon juice, sherry and almonds or capers. Sprinkle with paprika and parsley and chives. Serve on buttered, toasted English muffins, buttered toast or soft rolls (centers scooped out, buttered and toasted in 400° oven until crisp).
Serves 12

HOW TO COOK SWEETBREADS

2 pounds sweetbreads
ice water
1/4 cup lemon juice
1 teaspoon salt
1 carrot and 1 celery rib, cut up
1 onion, chopped
6 parsley sprigs
2 thyme sprigs
1 bay leaf, crumbled
8 peppercorns
2 cups dry white wine
water to cover

Soak sweetbreads in ice water several hours or overnight. Drain. Place in saucepan with all other ingredients, bring to gentle boil and simmer 10 to 15 minutes depending upon size. Cool in liquid, cover and refrigerate overnight. Remove skin, fat and membrane and break into 1-1/2-inch pieces. Strain cooking liquid and reserve. Sweetbreads freeze well up to 2 months. Place in jar and cover with cooking liquid up to 1 inch from top.

chafing dish

LAMB KIDNEYS IN MADEIRA SAUCE

2 pounds lamb kidneys
6 tablespoons olive oil
1-1/4 cups minced onions
1 teaspoon finely minced garlic
1 bay leaf, broken
2 tablespoons flour
1/2 cup chicken stock
3 tablespoons each minced parsley and
　 ground ham
1/2 teaspoon salt
1/4 teaspoon pepper
1/2 cup Madeira

Slice kidneys in half lengthwise and then across. Cover with cold water and bring to boil. Remove from heat and let stand 1 minute. Drain and rinse; let drain until almost dry. Heat 4 tablespoons of the oil and sauté onion, garlic and bay leaf, stirring often, until onion is transparent but not brown. Sprinkle with flour, cook and stir 3 minutes and gradually add stock. Cook and stir until thickened, add parsley and set aside. Heat remaining oil and quickly sauté kidneys, sprinkling with salt and pepper while they cook, 5 minutes or until evenly browned. Do not overcook. Add Madeira, stir to scrape up any brown bits on bottom of skillet and add reserved onion sauce. Reheat, adjust seasonings and transfer to chafing dish. Serve as side dish or with cocktail picks.
Serves 10 to 12 or makes approximately
　 60 buffet servings

CRAB MELBA

4 tablespoons butter
1/3 cup flour
2 cups half-and-half
2 tablespoons tomato paste or catsup
1/2 cup grated sharp Cheddar or Gruyère cheese
1-1/2 teaspoons paprika
1/2 teaspoon garlic powder
1/8 teaspoon cayenne pepper
1 tablespoon lemon juice
1/4 pound mushrooms, finely minced
1/4 cup finely minced green onions and tops
2 tablespoons butter
12 ounces each flaked crab meat and
　 minced lobster or shrimp
3 tablespoons minced pimiento
2 tablespoons dry sherry

Melt butter until bubbly. Sprinkle with flour; cook and stir 3 minutes. Gradually add half-and-half. Cook and stir until smooth and thickened. Add tomato paste, cheese, seasonings and lemon juice; cook and stir to melt cheese. Sauté mushrooms and onions in butter 5 minutes and add to cream sauce. With fork stir in crab and lobster or shrimp and pimiento. Reheat without boiling, add sherry and adjust seasonings. Transfer to chafing dish. Serve with water crackers or melba rounds.
Makes approximately 50 buffet servings

PORK BITS

1 pound lean pork, cut in 1-inch cubes
2 tablespoons soy sauce
1 teaspoon pressed garlic
1/4 teaspoon each black pepper and sugar
1/8 teaspoon powdered ginger

Mix pork well with other ingredients and let stand 1 hour. Spread on large shallow baking pan in single layer and bake in a 325° oven 1 hour, turning several times. Pour off any fat and transfer to chafing dish. Serve with cocktail picks.
Makes 4 dozen

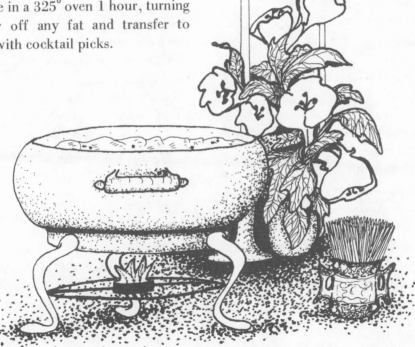

chafing dish

SHRIMP AND ARTICHOKES

1 pound cooked shrimp
2 packages frozen artichoke hearts, cooked
  and marinated (page 148)
1/2 pound small mushrooms
1 teaspoon finely minced garlic
2 tablespoons each olive oil and butter
1/2 teaspoon each salt and oregano
1/4 teaspoon pepper
1/16 teaspoon cayenne pepper
2 tablespoons lemon juice
1 basket cherry tomatoes
1/2 cup minced parsley
1 teaspoon freshly grated lemon peel

Combine shrimp and artichoke hearts with some of
the marinade. Set aside at room temperature.
Remove stems from mushrooms (save for soup
stock) and sauté mushroom caps and garlic in oil
and butter 4 to 5 minutes, sprinkling with seasonings and turning often. Add lemon juice and adjust
to taste with salt and pepper. Drain shrimp and
artichoke hearts and add to the mushrooms with
the cherry tomatoes. Reheat and transfer to chafing dish. Sprinkle with parsley and lemon peel.
Serve with cocktail picks.
Makes 40 to 50 buffet servings

CHICKEN LIVERS AND GIZZARDS

1/2 pound chicken livers, cut in bite-sized pieces
1/4 pound or more chicken gizzards,
  scored and sliced
2 tablespoons each butter and oil
1 teaspoon finely minced garlic
1 pound pork link sausages, cooked and
  cut into thirds
1/2 cup sliced water chestnuts
3/4 cup diagonally sliced celery
1 to 2 teaspoons minced ginger root
1 cup chicken or pork stock
1 to 2 tablespoons soy sauce
1/2 teaspoon salt
1/4 teaspoon pepper
1 tablespoon cornstarch
3 tablespoons water
minced parsley or Chinese parsley* sprigs

*See glossary

Sauté livers and gizzards in butter and oil to
brown, adding garlic last 2 minutes. Add sausage,
water chestnuts, celery, ginger, stock, soy sauce,
salt and pepper. Cover and cook 10 minutes. Dissolve cornstarch in water and add. Cook and stir
until thickened. Adjust seasonings and transfer to
chafing dish. Sprinkle with minced parsley or garnish with Chinese parsley. Serve with cocktail picks
for buffet, with rice for supper or as a brunch
accompaniment.
Makes approximately 50 buffet servings

PANNEQUETS

2 eggs, beaten
1 cup flour
1 cup milk or stock to complement the filling
1 tablespoon each brandy and melted butter
1/2 teaspoon salt

Fillings
crab triangles (page 114)
mushroom duxelle (page 12)
tomato-ham duxelle (page 12)

Combine ingredients, cover and refrigerate at least 2 hours. Stir well and pour 1 tablespoon into each of the 7 heated and buttered sections of pannequet pan (Swedish pancake pan). Cook on one side only until golden and transfer to rack, stacking and keeping warm in slow oven. Spread uncooked side with filling and roll tightly, tucking in edges. Place seam side down in chafing dish and drizzle with a little melted butter. Serve with cocktail picks.
Makes approximately 3 dozen

EASY CHAFING DISH SUGGESTIONS

• Combine and heat 2 cans frozen (defrosted) lobster bisque or shrimp, or combination, 1/2 cup milk, 1-1/2 cups grated Cheddar or Emmenthaler cheese and 2 crushed garlic cloves. Just before serving add 1/4 cup dry sherry. Serve with crusty French bread chunks.
• Heat 1 can frozen (defrosted) shrimp bisque, 8 ounces cream cheese cut in bits, 3 tablespoons chopped black olives with curry powder and Worcestershire sauce to taste. Serve with crackers.
• Bake 2 pounds pork link sausages in pan with rack 40 minutes in 325° oven, turning once to brown evenly and cook out fat. Cool and cut into thirds to make approximately 6 dozen buffet servings. Heat 1 cup each dark or light brown sugar and dark rum, add sausages and simmer 30 minutes. Cool and reheat the next day. Or: Combine and heat 8 ounces jellied cranberry sauce, 12 ounces chili sauce, 1 tablespoon lemon juice, 1/8 teaspoon cayenne pepper and 1 lemon, thinly sliced. Add sausages and simmer 1 hour. Both recipes can be made with cocktail franks or cut-up hot dogs or linguica sausage.

fireside

firepot

fondue

barbecue

FIRESIDE

• When a host wishes to honor guests in a special way, he may ask them to do the cooking—not in his sacrosanct kitchen, but in groups of eight or less in front of the fireplace or around electric skillets or fancy hot pots in the living room, dining room or patio.

• Though the guests do the cooking, the chef's role is still vital, for he or she must prepare the setting, utensils, sauces, seasonings and garnishes as well as cut, slice and attractively arrange the delicacies to be cooked. Luckily this can be done well ahead of time.

• The international "friendship dishes" such as fondues, raclettes, firepots, sin sul lo and mizutaki have long added an extra fillip of fun and intimacy for entertaining.

RACLETTE
Swiss Origin

2- or 3-pound block or wedge of any creamy white natural cheese (Raclette, Fontina, Swiss, Gruyère or Samsoe)
2 small, unpeeled new potatoes per person
2 white onions, thinly sliced
1 cup white vinegar
1/2 teaspoon salt
1/4 teaspoon dill weed
1-1/2 teaspoons sugar
sliced sweet and dill pickles
freshly ground pepper

Remove rind from cheese. Boil potatoes and keep warm until serving time. Marinate onion slices for 1 hour in a mixture of vinegar, salt, dill and sugar; cover and chill until ready to serve. Place cheese block in a heavy, shallow pan and set on the hearth near the fire so that it gradually melts. (You will learn to judge correct proximity after you have done this a few times.) Provide each guest with a heavy plate, large spoon and dinner fork. As cheese melts, guests scrape a spoonful from the liquid area and spread it on top of the potato, sprinkling with pepper. Serve with the marinated onions, pickles, crusty French bread, tossed green salad and wine. If you do not have a fireplace, the cheese may be prepared in an oven. Place block of cheese in a heavy pan and broil about 4 inches from heat. Serve at once. Repeat broiling when guests are ready for more cheese.
Serves 6 to 8

firepot

ORIENTAL FIREPOTS

Simmering broth, a favorite Oriental cooking medium, not only adds flavor to the meat and vegetables cooked therein, but picks up their piquancy for a delicious second-course soup to which bean thread noodles have been added.

If one intends to entertain with at-the-table cooking Oriental style more than once, it's well worth acquiring attractive gadgetry available in any Chinese houseware's store: elaborate firepot, bamboo chopsticks or small tongs, tiny wire baskets with handles, individual small dishes for dipping sauces and bowls for rice and soup, Oriental platters or shallow baskets, and special cruets.

For the following firepot recipes, provide chopsticks and tiny wire dipping baskets for guests. Let them select the vegetables or meat they want from a beautifully arranged platter and cook them in the simmering broth to the desired doneness. Around the firepot arrange tiny bowls of sauces and condiments in which guests dip the cooked morsels.

Sin sul lo (Korean for angel pot dish) differs from the other methods in that the guests do not select their own raw tidbits to cook. The host loads the pot with a prearranged assortment; the guests only remove with chopsticks what suits their fancy.

MONGOLIAN FIREPOT

leg of lamb, thinly sliced
vegetables from Chinese firepot
Chinese parsley* for garnish

Broth
1-1/2 to 2 cups beef or lamb broth per person
2 slices ginger root
1 garlic clove, halved

Dipping sauces and condiments
Mix any of the following combinations and serve in individual small bowls.
- Soy sauce, toasted sesame seeds, finely chopped peanuts
- Soy sauce, sake or dry sherry, pepper, crushed garlic, minced ginger root and green onions
- Hoisin sauce*
- Aji oil*—a must

*See glossary

Arrange lamb and vegetable selections decoratively on large platter. Garnish with parsley, cover with saran wrap and refrigerate until serving time. Bring broth to boil, add ginger root and garlic, lower heat and simmer 10 minutes. Transfer to hotpot.

CHINESE FIREPOT

tender cut of beef, very thinly sliced
chicken breasts cut into strips
halved chicken livers and/or scored and
    sliced gizzards
firm white fish cut in 1-inch cubes
halved shrimp
oysters and/or clams
squid cut in half lengthwise
Chinese cabbage, iceberg lettuce and/or
    spinach cut in strips
watercress
cucumbers, peeled, seeded and cut into strips
pea pods
sliced water chestnuts and bamboo shoots
firm bean curd* cut in 1/2-inch cubes
Chinese parsley* for garnish

Broth
1-1/2 to 2 cups chicken broth per person
2 slices ginger root
1 clove garlic, halved
2 to 3 softened, sliced dried forest mushrooms*
1/2 cup chopped green onions

Cruets of:
soy sauce
oyster sauce
sake or sherry
vinegar

Small bowls of condiments
minced green onion
minced ginger root
minced garlic
sliced pickled red ginger*
hoisin sauce*
plum sauce*

eggs, one per person
softened bean thread noodles*

*See glossary

Arrange a selection of meats and vegetables and the bean curd decoratively on large platter. Garnish with parsley, cover with saran wrap and refrigerate until serving time. Bring broth to boil, add ginger root, garlic, mushrooms and green onions, lower heat and simmer 10 minutes. Transfer to hotpot. Eggs are beaten in individual bowls to be used as a dip. After individual cooking has ended add bean thread noodles to broth and simmer until tender. Ladle noodles and broth into individual bowls containing beaten egg.

firepot

JAPANESE MIZUTAKI

tender cut of beef, very thinly sliced
chicken breasts cut into strips
sliced fresh mushrooms
green onions cut in 2-inch lengths
Chinese cabbage and/or spinach cut in strips
carrots cut in long, very thin strips
sliced Oriental eggplant
celery sliced on diagonal
sliced water chestnuts and bamboo shoots
watercress
firm bean curd* cut in 1-inch cubes

For garnish
chrysanthemum leaves
matsuba* or parsley sprigs

Broth
1-1/2 to 2 cups chicken broth per person
1/2 ounce kombu* (optional)

cooked pearl rice to be served in individual bowls
softened bean thread noodles*

Arrange meat, chicken, vegetable selections and bean curd decoratively on large platter. Garnish with chrysanthemum leaves and matsuba or parsley. Cover with saran wrap and refrigerate until serving time. Bring broth to boil, add kombu, lower heat and simmer 10 minutes. Discard kombu before transferring broth to hotpot. Guests cook their own morsels in broth and then dip them in any of the following sauces. After individual cooking has ended add bean thread noodles, simmer until tender and serve with broth.

Variation
Substitute clams and shrimp for beef and chicken; add gingko nuts.

Dipping sauces and condiments
Combine several of the following suggested mixtures and serve in individual small bowls.
• Soy sauce, lime juice, sugar.
• Soy sauce, toasted sesame seeds, rice vinegar*, corn oil, sesame oil.*
• Ground sesame seed (paste)*, white miso*, dashi*.
• Dashi*, soy sauce, lemon juice.
• Wasabi*.
• Grated daikon*.

*See glossary

KOREAN SIN SUL LO

daikon*, thinly sliced
Chinese cabbage and/or spinach cut in strips
sliced fresh mushrooms
firm bean curd* cut in 1-inch cubes
thinly sliced tender beef
sliced scallops and/or shrimp
chicken breast cut in thin strips
egg garni*
pine nuts
slivered green onions
1-1/2 to 2 cups beef broth per person
softened bean thread noodles*

In order given, layer vegetables and meats in hot-pot. Bring broth to boil and carefully pour into hotpot, so as not to disturb the layers. Bring back to gentle boil, cover and simmer 7 minutes. Provide chopsticks with which guests select cooked morsels. At end of meal add bean thread noodles, cook until tender and serve with the broth.

Dipping sauce
Mixture of: soy sauce, toasted sesame seeds, sugar, water, salt, pepper and Tabasco or Aji oil*.

Condiment
kim chee*

*See glossary

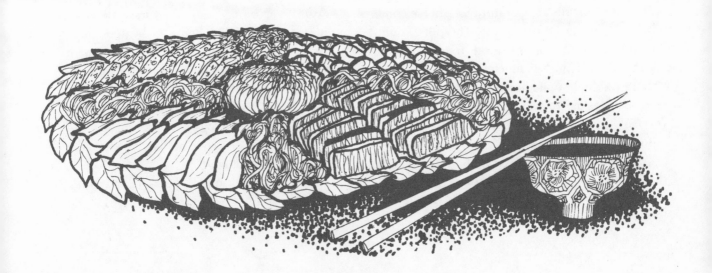

fondue

FONDUES

In French the word *fondant* means melting, juicy, luscious—a most apt trio of adjectives to describe the many dishes called fondues in which melted cheese plays a key role. Here we're only concerned with those where pieces of bread or other morsels are skewered on long forks and dipped in a pot of melted cheese seasoned and thinned to the right consistency with wine and Kirsch (or other brandy). A recent trend has developed also to call small chunks of meat cooked in hot oil with similar equipment fondues. They, too, are juicy and luscious, and, if the meat is tender, literally melt in your mouth.

No host-chef should be without a fancy fondue pot and fondue forks. A heavy, special fondue pot or pot with a shallow base for hot water, like a double boiler, controls the temperature for cheese fondues that tend to curdle if too hot. The pot should be directly on the heat for meat fondues, though, because the oil must be much hotter.

Bread should be cubed, leaving the crust on one face of each piece. Wine and brandy should be of good quality. If the consistency in the pot is just right, the coated morsel will trail strings of cheese as it is removed. A quick twirl and a flourish, with the finesse of an Italian eating spaghetti, are required to overcome the reluctance of the cheese to leave the pot.

CHEESE FONDUE

garlic
6 ounces each Emmenthaler and Gruyère
  cheese, grated
1 tablespoon potato flour or cornstarch
1/4 teaspoon each salt and white pepper
1/8 teaspoon nutmeg
1 cup good quality light dry white wine
2 tablespoons Kirsch or brandy

Rub bottom and sides of heavy earthenware casserole, fondue pot or chafing dish with cut garlic. Toss cheeses with potato flour or cornstarch and seasonings. Pour wine into pot and heat until bubbles start rising to surface. Do not boil. With wooden fork or spoon stir in a handful of cheese at a time. Stir constantly until cheese is melted. Adjust seasonings and add Kirsch or brandy. Once ingredients are blended and heated, do not cook further; adjust heat accordingly. Serve with:

• Chunks of sourdough bread, Italian bread or
  other crusty bread
• Cubes of ham, cooked chicken, lobster,
  shrimp, crab legs
• Raw vegetables such as carrots, zucchini,
  celery sticks
• Fruits such as apples, pears, cherry tomatoes

BEEF FONDUE

beef tenderloin cut into 3/4-inch cubes
   (1 pound yields approximately 40 cubes)
lettuce
oil and clarified butter*

Sauce Selections
hollandaise, béarnaise, mousseline
horseradish sauce
sour cream dill sauce
yoghurt sauce
aioli
tomato sauce
chili sauce, mayonnaise and lemon juice
curry sauce
whiskey sauce
chutney sauce
herb sauce
homemade mayonnaise
caper mayonnaise
anchovy sauce
butter with lemon juice
burnt butter

*See glossary

Let meat stand at room temperature 1 hour before serving. Arrange on lettuce. Place condiments in small bowls. Fill fondue pot with oil or half oil and half clarified butter and keep at 375°. Provide a plate, fork and bamboo skewer or fondue fork for each guest.

Fondue Variations
Instead of beef substitute one or more of the following:
chicken breasts, cut into bite-sized pieces
firm white fish, cut in cubes
halved shrimp and/or scallops
carrot flowers
halved or quartered mushrooms
green pepper wedges
green onions in 2-inch pieces
green or wax beans in 1-1/2-inch pieces
cauliflower or broccoli flowerets
cubed eggplant
zucchini strips
sliced sunchokes

LAMB FONDUE

Follow directions for beef fondue. Choose from list of sauces or the following:
• Olive oil, lemon juice and garlic (lamb marinade).
• Yoghurt mixed with shredded zucchini, minced onions and cumin.
• Tomato sauce with cumin, Tabasco and extra basil added.

fondue

BAGNA CAUDA FONDUE

1/4 pound butter
1/2 cup olive oil
4 cloves garlic, finely minced
8 anchovy fillets, finely chopped
bite-sized pieces of raw beef, cauliflower, green
    pepper, celery, carrot, mushroom quarters,
    artichoke bottoms and endive

Heat together in a chafing dish or fondue pot (not candle type) the butter, olive oil, garlic and anchovies. Let guests dip meat and vegetables into hot mixture until cooked to desired doneness. Serve with French bread.

CHICKEN CHEESE FONDUE

6 ounces each Emmenthaler and Gruyère
    cheese, grated
1 tablespoon potato flour or cornstarch
1 10-1/2-ounce can condensed cream of
    chicken soup
1/2 to 1 teaspoon pressed garlic
1 to 2 teaspoons curry powder
1/4 to 1/2 teaspoon powdered ginger
1/4 teaspoon white pepper
1/2 cup sour cream

Toss cheese with flour or cornstarch. Heat soup, garlic and seasonings and stir to blend well. Add cheeses a handful at a time. When cheeses are melted, blend in sour cream. Adjust seasonings. Reduce heat.

OMELET PANCAKES

Vegetables
bean sprouts
shredded lettuce, Chinese cabbage, spinach,
  Swiss chard, bok choy

Accompaniments
chopped mushrooms, green pepper, tomato,
  water chestnuts, bamboo shoots, chives,
  green onions, Chinese parsley*
diced ham, poultry
bits of fish, shellfish
finely minced ginger root, garlic
shredded daikon*

Condiments
mayonnaise
catsup
mild and hot mustard
soy sauce
Aji oil*

Presentation
basket of eggs
bowl of flour with 1 tablespoon measuring spoon
bowl of water with 1 tablespoon measuring spoon
cruet of corn oil
electric skillet
spatula
plate, fork, medium-sized bowl and chopsticks
  or fork for mixing batter for each guest

*See glossary

Shred vegetables and arrange attractively on tray and mound accompaniments around them. Place bowls of condiments on table alongside basket of eggs and bowls of flour and water. Each guest mixes 1 tablespoon each flour and water to a paste and then beats in 1 egg. He adds vegetables and accompaniments at will. Oil is heated in electric skillet and guests cook their own 4- to 6-inch pancake until golden on each side.

barbecue

BARBECUE

Skewer cooking on a charcoal grill well removed from the hors d'oeuvre table offers two definite advantages: to help disperse the inevitable crowd around the main table and to lighten the pressure on the kitchen. An assistant chef should take charge, though he may find his job easy if eager guests enter into the fun of cooking their own 1/2-inch appetizer bits, 2 or 3 speared on a small wood skewer.

For supper, 3/4-inch bits, perhaps 4 or 5 for each skewer, can be cooked en masse and arranged on a platter with other foods and garnishes.

Shellfish, firm fish, meats (and their innards), poultry and game (including livers, hearts and gizzards)—even frog legs—are delicious barbecued if properly marinated, frequently basted, and not overcooked (especially small morsels). Five inches, at least, is required between glowing coals and meat, and skewers must be constantly turned. Arrange skewers around the grill's periphery for easy manipulation and retrieval.

One pound of meat or poultry yields approximately 50 1/2-inch pieces or 30 3/4-inch pieces.

MARINADES

Turn foods often while marinating. While cooking, unless otherwise specified, baste frequently with marinade, strained if desired. If marinade contains no oil, add 1/4 cup salad or olive oil.

Marinating time varies:
- Fish and shellfish, 30 to 40 minutes.
- Frog legs, 1 hour.
- Ham, 1 to 2 hours.
- Cut-up poultry and game birds, 1 to 3 hours.
- Game meats and meats (and their innards), 2 to 4 hours.
- Large pieces of meat such as flank or skirt steak, whole chicken, game hens and boned leg of lamb, 4 to 6 hours or overnight.
- Cheaper cuts of meat such as chuck steak, at least overnight.

SEAFOOD MARINADE

- Combine equal parts olive oil and lemon juice or white wine.
- Combine 1/4 cup each lemon juice and olive oil, 1 pressed garlic clove, 1/2 teaspoon salt, 1/4 teaspoon white pepper and 1 sprig each thyme and rosemary.

MARINADES FOR LAMB, BEEF AND THEIR INNARDS

• *Red wine vinegar:* Combine 1/3 cup olive oil, 2 tablespoons red wine vinegar, 4 slices onion, 1 sliced garlic clove, 1/2 teaspoon salt, 1/4 teaspoon each pepper and paprika, 2 thyme sprigs and 8 mint sprigs.

• *Dill:* Combine 1/3 cup olive oil, 2 tablespoons lemon juice, 1/2 teaspoon salt, 1/4 teaspoon pepper, 2 halved garlic cloves and 3 to 4 tablespoons minced dill weed.

• *Yoghurt (Pakistan):* Combine 1/2 cup plain yoghurt, 3 tablespoons minced onion, 1/2 teaspoon minced garlic, 1/2 teaspoon salt, 1/4 teaspoon each crumbled dried hot chili pepper, cumin and powdered ginger and 1/8 teaspoon each ground cardamom, pepper, cinnamon and powdered cloves. This is also good with chicken.

• *Mint (Mideast):* Combine 1/4 cup each olive oil and lemon juice, 1 teaspoon salt, 1/2 teaspoon pepper, 2 finely minced garlic cloves and 1/3 cup minced mint.

• *Oregano (Mideast):* Combine 1/4 cup each olive oil and lemon juice, 1 teaspoon salt, 3/4 to 1 teaspoon oregano and 1/4 teaspoon pepper.

• *Tomato:* Combine 1 cup chopped canned or peeled fresh tomatoes, 1/4 cup grated onion, 1 crumbled bay leaf, 1/4 teaspoon each pepper, oregano and sugar, 3 tablespoons minced parsley and 1/4 teaspoon cinnamon (optional). Baste with plain olive oil.

• *Oyster sauce (Oriental):* Combine 3 tablespoons oyster sauce*, 2 tablespoons each corn oil and chopped green onion, 1 tablespoon soy sauce and 1/2 teaspoon minced garlic. Cut meat in paper-thin slices. Skewer with mushrooms and water chestnuts, if desired.

GAME AND POULTRY MARINADES

For venison, moose or caribou: Combine 1/2 cup red wine, 1 tablespoon lemon juice or wine vinegar, 2 tablespoons minced onion, 1 tablespoon minced carrot, 1 crumbled bay leaf, 2 parsley sprigs, 2 thyme sprigs, 2 whole cloves and 4 peppercorns, crushed.

For poultry and game birds and meats:
• Combine 1/2 cup olive oil, 1 teaspoon salt, 1/4 teaspoon pepper, 1/2 teaspoon Worcestershire sauce and 1 teaspoon minced garlic.
• Combine 1/3 cup lemon juice, 1 teaspoon salt and 1/2 to 1 teaspoon chili powder.
• Combine, 1/4 cup each soy sauce and chicken stock, 2 tablespoons each sherry and wine vinegar, 1/2 teaspoon sugar, 1/2 apple, peeled and grated, 1 clove minced garlic and 1/4 teaspoon sesame oil*.

barbecue

PORK MARINADE

Combine 2/3 cup soy sauce, 1/3 cup sake or dry sherry, 1 teaspoon brown sugar, 1 minced garlic clove, 1/2 teaspoon sesame oil*, and 1/4 cup toasted sesame seeds (optional).

ALL-PURPOSE ORIENTAL MARINADES

• Combine 1/4 cup soy sauce, 3 tablespoons sake, dry sherry or whiskey, 1 tablespoon sugar, 3 slices ginger root and 1/2 teaspoon each five spices powder* and softened and minced dried tangerine peel*.

• Combine 1/3 cup soy sauce, 3 tablespoons sugar, 2 tablespoons vinegar, 2 to 3 pressed cloves garlic, 1 to 2 teaspoons finely minced ginger root and 1/2 teaspoon sesame oil*. Baste with corn oil and sake or dry sherry.

• Combine 1/4 cup each soy sauce and white wine, 2 teaspoons sugar, 3 tablespoons minced green onion and tops and 2 to 3 tablespoons toasted sesame seeds, crushed.

*See glossary

HAM MARINADE

Combine and cook 5 minutes: 1/4 cup brown sugar, 2 tablespoons vinegar, 2 to 3 teaspoons Dijon-style mustard and 1/2 teaspoon finely minced garlic. Add 1/4 cup pineapple juice. Alternate ham and pineapple chunks on skewer.

MORE BARBECUE IDEAS
• Wrap thinly sliced beef around water chestnut.
• Dip oysters in butter and bread crumbs with or without grated Parmesan cheese.
• Wrap halved scallops in blanched bacon strip and skewer alternately with shrimp. After broiling sprinkle with pepper.
• Combine equal amounts crumbled Gorgonzola cheese and cream cheese. Add half-and-half to just soften, salt, white pepper, cayenne, minced parsley, minced chives, and minced prosciutto (optional) to taste. Stuff mushroom caps and sprinkle with paprika. Thread on skewers stuffed side up and broil over charcoal 6 minutes or until stuffing is heated.

SUGGESTED FOODS TO SKEWER
WITH MEAT, FISH, POULTRY, GAME

halved or whole water chestnuts
lichee nuts
oysters dipped in lemon juice and butter
oysters wrapped in bacon
blanched green pepper
unpeeled orange eighths
small parboiled or pickled onions
fresh pineapple
cherry tomatoes, ripe or green
seedless grapes
unpeeled eggplant
small parboiled potato balls
mushrooms
pitted ripe olives
pimiento-stuffed olives
cubes of cheese wrapped in thinly sliced ham
squares of bacon (especially good with
  kidney, heart, liver)
apple cubes
parboiled yam or sweet potato balls
buttered banana chunks
zucchini chunks
lobster (with beef)

YAKITORI

1/2 cup each soy sauce and Mirin*
3 slices ginger root
2 cloves garlic, halved
1 pound chicken meat cut into 1-inch cubes
1/4 pound chicken livers, cut into thirds
  (optional)

Presentation
finely shredded daikon* seasoned to taste with
  powdered ginger and pepper
dry mustard mixed with hot water to
  make paste

*See glossary

Combine soy sauce, Mirin, ginger root and garlic. Let stand 4 hours or more. Add chicken and optional livers and marinate 20 minutes. Discard ginger and garlic. Skewer 2 pieces chicken and/or liver. Broil over hot coals, basting and turning, 6 to 8 minutes. Do not overcook. Serve with bowls of seasoned daikon and mustard sauce.
Makes 24 buffet servings

buffet

HINTS FOR LARGE BUFFET

- Choose food for color, texture and especially variety. Foods must complement each other.
- Foods that can be made ahead or frozen will facilitate preparation the day of the party.
- Do not plan many cold canapes unless time and help is available.
- Choose recipes that can be easily doubled or tripled.
- Keep in mind which foods must be kept chilled and how much refrigerator space is available.
- Do not plan more broiled or baked foods than oven or ovens can handle.
- If serving sliced ham, turkey, beef or other meat always be sure the slices are *very* thin. Hunks of meat and uneven thick slices are unattractive and awkward to handle. If unable to slice thinly at home, ask your butcher to do so.
- Count on approximately 14 bites per person; some guests leave early, some stay on. Remember to plan for helpers and entertainers.
- Plan table arrangement so guests can go all the way around the table. Make up a plan ahead and if serving a very large group, place name of dish on spot where it is to be placed so helpers can follow arrangement plan.
- If possible, place some dishes in other parts of the house and set up barbecues to encourage guests to circulate.
- Provide 6- to 7-inch plates or hors d'oeuvre trays (available in paper), napkins and perhaps forks.
- Check replenishing and garnishing of dishes; never let an empty platter remain on the table.
- Plan enough passing foods so guests need not crowd around table.
- If serving soup, choose a light soup that needs no spoon and serve in mugs from a tureen.
- Choose simple desserts that do not require plates or bowls.
- Helpers should arrive at least one hour before party is to begin.
- For 100 guests plan to have at least one helper in the kitchen, one to arrange and pass hot and cold appetizers, and one to replenish buffet, empty ashtrays and help in kitchen.

buffet

MARINATED VEGETABLES

Mix 1 cup olive oil, 1/3 cup wine vinegar, 1 teaspoon minced oregano or tarragon, 1/2 teaspoon salt and 1/4 teaspoon pepper. In this mixture marinate raw mushrooms chilled for several days or cooked artichoke bottoms, raw string beans or plum tomatoes several hours. For tomatoes add 1 tablespoon sugar to marinade. Before serving sprinkle vegetables with minced parsley.

RAW VEGETABLE PLATTER

Although simple, chilled raw vegetables are among the most popular and nutritious hors d'oeuvre. In selecting the vegetables, keep in mind variety in both the colors and shapes. In addition to the ubiquitous carrot and celery sticks include some vegetables usually not eaten raw: cauliflowerets, tiny green asparagus tips, Belgian endive leaves, broccoli stems pared and cut into rounds, zucchini, turnip sticks, green beans, mushroom slices, fennel sticks, small Brussels sprouts, jicama sticks, sunchoke slices, and avocado balls rubbed with lemon juice and speared on picks.

PICKLED VEGETABLES

1-1/2 cups each water and vinegar
1/2 cup olive oil
3 onions, sliced
2 tablespoons sugar
1 tablespoon salt
1 teaspoon each celery seed and mustard seed
1/2 teaspoon crushed dried chili pepper (optional)
vegetables

For vegetables select a mixture of any of the following: small trimmed artichoke hearts, celery hearts or ribs, Brussels sprouts, cauliflowerets whole green onions with 2 inches of top, small white onions, asparagus spears, carrot and zucchini sticks or slices, eggplant cut in julienne, whole or sliced mushrooms, broccoli flowerets.
Combine ingredients and bring to boil. Boil 5 minutes, add vegetables, bring back to boil and cook until just tender-crisp. Cool and chill several hours. Remove vegetables and arrange on serving platter. Sprinkle with minced dill, basil, parsley or chives.

SUNCHOKE SALAD

1/2 cup olive oil
3 tablespoons tarragon vinegar
2 tablespoons lemon juice
1/2 teaspoon each Dijon-style mustard and salt
1/4 teaspoon white pepper

2 cups thinly sliced cooked sunchokes (page 89)
1 cup thinly sliced red onions

Presentation
romaine or iceberg lettuce, broken
1/2 cup crisp crumbled cooked bacon
cherry tomatoes
hard-cooked egg slices
parsley sprigs

Combine oil, vinegar, lemon juice, mustard, salt and pepper. Toss sunchokes and onions in dressing, cover and chill 1 to 2 hours.
Toss sunchokes, onions and dressing with lettuce and bacon. Season if needed with salt and pepper. Mound on serving platter and surround with tomatoes, egg slices and parsley.
Serves 6

WATERCRESS CREAM MOLD

8 ounces cream cheese, softened
2 ounces Gorgonzola cheese, room temperature
2 tablespoons horseradish
1/2 cup mayonnaise
3 tablespoons lemon juice
1 teaspoon gelatin
2 tablespoons cold water
1-1/2 cups chopped watercress
1 cup heavy cream, whipped

shredded lettuce
watercress sprigs

Combine cheeses, horseradish, mayonnaise and lemon juice. Soften gelatin in cold water and dissolve over hot water. Cool. Add to cheese mixture with watercress. Fold in cream and turn into lightly oiled 6-cup mold. Cover and chill 6 hours. Turn out onto lettuce and garnish with watercress sprigs. Serve as salad or with crackers or melba rounds.
Makes 8 salad servings, 30 buffet servings

buffet

AVOCADO RING WITH FRUIT

2 envelopes gelatin
1/2 cup cold water
3/4 cup boiling water
2 tablespoons lemon juice
1/2 pint sour cream
1/4 teaspoon salt
2 large avocados, puréed
2 cups fresh grapefruit sections
orange dressing (recipe follows)

Soften gelatin in cold water. Pour boiling water over and stir until dissolved. Add lemon juice and cool. With a whisk, carefully blend in sour cream. Chill mixture until partially set. Beat thickened mixture with a rotary beater until light and fluffy; add avocado purée and salt and beat again. Fold in grapefruit pieces and turn into an oiled 6-cup salad ring mold. Chill until firm. Unmold on large platter and place a small bowl of orange dressing in center. Surround ring with cut-up fresh fruit and sprinkle the fruit with pomegranate seeds.
Serves 8 to 10

ORANGE DRESSING

1/2 pint sour cream
1/2 cup sifted powdered sugar
2 tablespoons orange juice
2 tablespoons orange-flavored liqueur
1 teaspoon grated orange peel

Combine ingredients, cover and chill.
Makes 1-1/2 cups

CELERIAC SALAD

Cut peeled celeriac into match-stick pieces. Leave raw or cook tender-crisp in boiling salted water. Marinate in French dressing, drain and combine with cream dressing, minced tarragon and lemon juice to taste. Or combine with vinaigrette sauce. Serve on romaine or iceberg lettuce.

SUGGESTIONS FOR BUFFET
CHEESE TRAYS FOR 12

- *Cheese Tray I*
Boursin with herbs (5 ounces)
Boursin with cracked pepper (5 ounces)
Swiss such as Appenzeller, Gruyère
    (8 to 12 ounces)
Havarti, Tilsit or Port Salut (8 to 12 ounces)
mild blue cheese such as Gorgonzola (8 ounces)

- *Cheese Tray II*
spiced cheese such as Leyden or Tilsit with
    caraway or cayenne
aged Cheddar
Monterey Jack
Brick
(2 to 3 pounds in all)

- *Cheese Tray III*
French Münster with or without parsley
Pipo crème (blue)
Chèvre or St. Marcellin
Provolone
(2 to 3 pounds in all)

Garnish trays with clusters of grapes.

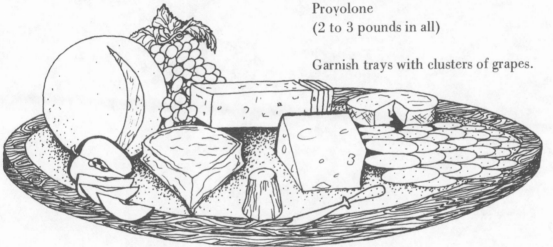

buffet

PICKLED HERRING

3 pounds herring, cleaned and soaked in
    cold water 2 hours
2 onions, thinly sliced
1 lemon, thinly sliced
1-1/2 cups white vinegar
1 cup water
2 bay leaves
4 each whole cloves and allspice
1 2-inch stick cinnamon
2 teaspoons peppercorns
1 teaspoon salt
1/2 teaspoon nutmeg
2 tablespoons salad oil

Presentation
parsley sprigs
sliced apples
sliced hard-cooked eggs
fresh or pickled cucumbers
sliced radishes or beets
small lettuce leaves
buttered firm dark bread

Cut herring into lengthwise fillets and then into
2-inch pieces. In a jar, layer herring, onion and
lemon. Boil vinegar, water and seasonings 5 minutes. Cool and mix in oil. Pour over herring, cover
and store in cool place 2 weeks.

Place herring on serving platter or in shallow bowl.
Garnish with parsley, apples, eggs, cucumbers and
radishes or beets. Guests spoon mixture and garnish onto lettuce and/or bread.

Makes approximately 50 buffet servings

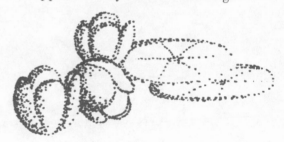

SEVICHE

1-1/2 pounds *very* fresh firm white fish, shredded
1 cup lime or lemon juice
2 tablespoons finely minced green pepper
3 tablespoons finely minced onion
1/4 cup olive or salad oil
1/2 teaspoon salt
1/4 teaspoon pepper
6 drops Tabasco
1/4 cup chopped fresh coriander*
1/2 cup peeled, seeded and finely
    chopped tomatoes
fresh coriander for garnish

*See glossary

Marinate fish in lime or lemon juice 3 hours in refrigerator, stirring often. Add remaining ingredients and chill. Just before serving check for salt, pepper and Tabasco. For hotter seviche, use finely minced aji or hot fresh peppers or dried hot red pepper flakes instead of Tabasco.
Place seviche in bowl and garnish with fresh coriander. Provide guests with a small fork and an oyster or scallop shell. Crusty French bread goes well with the fish.
Makes approximately 50 buffet servings

Variation with Scallops
To 1 pound thinly sliced and slivered scallops add 3/4 cup lime juice. Marinate 8 hours and add thinly sliced red onion, salt, pepper, chopped parsley and dried hot red pepper flakes to taste.

HAM AND PARSLEY IN ASPIC

2 tablespoons brandy
1 tablespoon minced parsley
3 peppercorns, crushed
2 whole allspice, crushed
12 ounces cooked ham cut into
    tiny cubes (2 cups)
3/4 cup finely minced parsley
3 cups Madeira jelly (page 17)

Presentation
parsley sprigs
homemade mayonnaise

Combine brandy, 1 tablespoon parsley, peppercorns and allspice. Pour over ham and marinate, tossing frequently, 3 to 4 hours. Drain and place in 1-quart mold that has been rinsed in cold water. Distribute parsley over ham and slowly pour in jelly. Cover and refrigerate 6 hours or overnight. Turn aspic onto serving platter and surround with ring of parsley sprigs. Serve with mayonnaise.
Makes approximately 25 buffet servings

buffet

CURRIED KIDNEY BEANS

1/4 pound butter
2 onions, chopped
2 green peppers, chopped
2 apples, chopped
2 teaspoons curry powder
2 28-ounce cans tomatoes
4 15-ounce cans kidney beans, drained
2 cups brown sugar
2 tablespoons white vinegar
salt and pepper to taste
grated Parmesan cheese

Melt butter and sauté onion, pepper, apple and curry powder until tender. Place tomatoes in a colander and squeeze until all liquid is removed (reserve liquid for other uses). Combine drained tomatoes with sautéed onion mixture, kidney beans, brown sugar, vinegar, salt and pepper in a casserole. Bake at 350° for 30 minutes. Sprinkle with Parmesan cheese before serving. Delicious with ham.
Serves 12

ZWIEBELKUCHEN
(Onion Pie)

1 recipe pizza dough (page 103)
2 pounds onions, diced (about 5 cups)
4 ounces lean bacon, minced
1 tablespoon butter
1/2 teaspoon salt
2 tablespoons flour
3 eggs, beaten
1-1/3 cups sour cream
1/2 pint creamed small curd cottage cheese
1 to 2 teaspoons caraway seeds
salt to taste
bits of butter and/or bacon

Sauté onions and bacon in butter 3 to 4 minutes to soften. Sprinkle with salt and flour, cook and stir 3 minutes and remove from heat. Cool slightly and add eggs, sour cream, cottage cheese and caraway seeds. Adjust seasonings with salt and set aside. After first rising of pizza dough, roll out 1/4 inch thick and place in a buttered 10-inch straight-sided pie tin. Trim edges even with rim of tin. Pour onion mixture in and dot with butter or bacon bits. Bake in 375° oven 1 hour or until top is golden and toothpick inserted in center comes out clean. Cool slightly and cut into wedges. May also be eaten at room temperature or may be reheated if wrapped loosely in foil.
Serves 10 to 12

TEPENADE SAUCE WITH EGGS

1 7-1/2-ounce can oil-packed tuna fish
4 to 6 anchovy fillets
3 tablespoons drained capers
3 garlic cloves, minced
20 medium pitted black olives
6 tablespoons lime juice
1/2 teaspoon black pepper
6 tablespoons or more olive oil
2 to 3 tablespoons brandy

Presentation
8 small hard-cooked eggs, halved
2 cups cauliflowerets
8 pitted black olives, halved
parsley sprigs

In blender purée tuna and its oil, anchovies and their oil, capers, garlic, olives, lime juice and pepper. Gradually blend in oil until sauce is the consistency of mayonnaise. Add brandy and adjust seasonings to taste. Refrigerate.
Arrange eggs around edge of platter alternately with several cauliflowerets. Place a bowl in center and fill with sauce. Place 2 teaspoons sauce on each egg half and top with olive half. Tuck sprigs of parsley around eggs. Guests help themselves to eggs and dip the cauliflowerets into the sauce. Remaining sauce keeps well if covered and refrigerated. Use as dip for other vegetables.
Makes 16 egg servings;
approximately 32 cauliflower servings

ZUCCHINI-SWISS CHARD FRITTATA

2 pounds small zucchini, thinly sliced
2 cups minced onion
2 to 3 cloves garlic, minced
2 to 3 tablespoons olive oil
1 small bunch Swiss chard, chopped
   (5 to 6 firmly packed cups)
1 teaspoon finely minced thyme
1/2 teaspoon each salt and finely minced
   sage and rosemary
3/4 cup minced parsley
10 eggs, well beaten and strained
1/2 pound grated Parmesan and/or Romano cheese

Sauté zucchini, onion and garlic in oil until zucchini is just tender-crisp. Add chard and cook and stir until chard is wilted, adding more oil if needed. Season and adjust to taste; add parsley and cool. Beat eggs and cheese, stir in zucchini mixture and blend well. Pour into 2 heavily buttered shallow baking pans approximately 12x7 inches. Bake in 350° oven 30 minutes or until toothpick inserted in center comes out clean. Cool slightly before cutting into squares. Serve warm or at room temperature. If making ahead, cover loosely and reheat just before serving.
Makes approximately 120 buffet servings

buffet

PISSALADIÈRE

1 recipe short crust pastry made with
   parsley (page 102)
1/4 cup each grated Parmesan and Gruyère cheese
1-1/2 cups minced onion
2 tablespoons butter
1 teaspoon minced garlic
2 teaspoons olive oil
4 large ripe tomatoes, peeled, seeded
   and chopped
1/2 teaspoon each sugar, salt and
   Worcestershire sauce
2 to 3 sprigs rosemary
1/4 teaspoon pepper
3 drops Tabasco
2 2-ounce cans flat anchovies
20 to 30 medium pitted black olives, halved
1 tablespoon olive oil

Roll 1/2 short crust pastry 1/4 inch thick and line a flan pan or other striaght-sided pan with removable bottom. Build edges up slightly and flute. Sprinkle with cheeses and chill. Sauté onion in butter, covered, until soft. Remove cover and let moisture cook away without browning. Cool. Sauté garlic in oil 3 minutes, add tomatoes and seasonings and cook over medium low heat, stirring occasionally, until reduced to 1-3/4 cups. Remove rosemary sprigs and purée mixture in blender. Reheat and adjust seasonings. If tomatoes were very juicy, thicken with paste of 1 teaspoon butter and 2 teaspoons flour. Sauce should be thick but not stiff.

Arrange minced onions on cheeses and pour sauce over. Freeze if desired and wrap well. Store up to 2 months. Defrost. Decorate sauce with anchovies and olive halves in spoke pattern, brush with oil and bake in 450° oven 25 minutes or until crust is golden and filling set. Remove from pan as directed and cool slightly before cutting. May be served hot or at room temperature. May also be baked in ordinary pie plate and served directly from the plate. Cut in small wedges for buffet.

Makes 20 to 30 buffet servings

CHICKEN WINGS

4 pounds chicken wings
double recipe yakitori marinade (page 145)
2 eggs, beaten
2 tablespoons dry sherry
seasoned bread crumbs

Remove tips (save for soup) from chicken wings and cut wings at joint. Marinate 2 to 3 hours. Dip in egg beaten with sherry, and then in bread crumbs. Place in one layer on shallow pan and refrigerate 1 hour or longer. Deep fry until golden and drain on paper toweling. Freeze if desired. Reheat in 350° oven.
Makes approximately 40 to 48

buffet

POACHED WHOLE SALMON

1 5- to 7-pound whole salmon
salt
1 lemon, sliced
1 onion, sliced
1 bay leaf, crumbled
4 peppercorns

Presentation
several bunches of parsley
flowers such as chrysanthemums,
    daisies or geraniums
lemon slices
minced parsley
hard-cooked eggs, whites and yolks
    sieved separately
artichoke heart halves
cherry tomatoes
lettuce cups filled with homemade mayonnaise

Wrap salmon in cheesecloth. Fill a poacher or kettle large enough for the salmon 3/4 full of water. For each quart of water add 1 tablespoon salt. Bring to rolling boil, lower salmon into the water and quickly place the lemon, onion, bay leaf and peppercorns on top. When water again boils continue cooking 5 minutes. Cool salmon in cooking liquid. Remove cheesecloth and skin. Cover and refrigerate.

Place salmon on large oval platter. Stuff mouth and cover tail with parsley sprigs. Arrange flowers on salmon; or decorate artistically with lemon slices, minced parsley and eggs. Arrange artichoke hearts and tomatoes around salmon alternately with lettuce cups. Serve with light rye crisp or water crackers.

Makes approximately 40 buffet servings

CRAB AND SHRIMP MOUSSE

2 cups tomato jelly (page 17)
1/2 pint sour cream
1 tablespoon lemon juice
2 tablespoons each finely minced
    pimiento-stuffed olives, celery and parsley
1 tablespoon finely minced green pepper (optional)
1/2 teaspoon each salt and Worcestershire sauce
4 to 6 drops Tabasco
10 ounces each whole shrimp and flaked crab
fish jelly (page 17) (optional)

Presentation
watercress
lemon slices
minced parsley
hard-cooked eggs, sliced

Cool tomato jelly slightly and add sour cream, lemon juice, olives, celery, parsley, green pepper and seasonings. Reserve 12 shrimp. Cut all remaining shrimp into small pieces and add with crab to tomato mixture. Adjust seasonings and pour into oiled mold. If desired line mold first with jelly made with fish stock or clam juice.
Unmold mousse on bed of watercress. Dip lemon slices in parsley and arrange around mousse alternately with eggs. Decorate top with whole shrimp.
Makes approximately 20 buffet servings

TUNA MOUSSE

2 envelopes gelatin
1/2 cup cold water
1/3 cup grated onion
3 tablespoons lemon juice
1 cup mayonnaise
1 pint sour cream
1/2 cup *finely* minced celery
1/4 cup minced parsley
1/2 teaspoon white pepper
4 7-ounce cans water-pack tuna fish,
    drained and finely flaked
aspic (pages 17-19)

Presentation
shredded lettuce
cherry tomatoes
lemon cucumber slices

Soften gelatin in cold water and dissolve over hot water. Combine with onion, lemon juice, mayonnaise, sour cream, celery, parsley and pepper. With fork, stir in tuna. Adjust seasonings, adding salt if needed. Choose method and decorations for working with aspics, using fish stock or clam juice as base for aspic. Fill a 6- to 8-cup (fish-shaped) mold. Chill 6 hours or overnight.
Unmold on lettuce and arrange tomatoes and cucumber around mousse.
Makes approximately 20 buffet servings

buffet

STEAK TARTARE

1 pound fat-free round steak, *freshly* ground
1/3 cup grated onion
1 teaspoon grated garlic
1 teaspoon salt
1/4 teaspoon pepper
1 egg white, slightly beaten

Presentation Suggestions
1 thin onion ring
1 raw egg yolk
minced parsley and chives
hard-cooked eggs, whites and yolks
   sieved separately
chopped green onions, white and tops separate
cross-cut slices of pimiento-stuffed olives
sliced black olives
minced gherkins
chopped toasted walnuts
capers
finely chopped anchovies
lumpfish caviar and minced onions
cocktail rye, pumpernickel, and/or dark rye

Combine ingredients, but do not handle more than necessary. Adjust seasonings and chill. Simplicity is the key to steak tartare. If guests prefer to mask the taste of the beef with highly seasoned ingredients, let them help themselves.

Mound meat on serving platter and form into flat dome shape. Press down in center to make a hollow, place onion ring around hollow and break the egg yolk into it. Choose 5 or 6 assorted garnishes and decorate the meat and the serving platter. Place basket of bread alongside.

Makes approximately 50 buffet servings

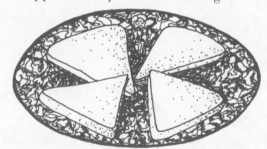

160

KIBBEE

1 pound leg of lamb with *no* fat
1 cup very-fine bulghur wheat
cold water to cover
1 teaspoon salt
1/4 teaspoon allspice
1/8 teaspoon each black and cayenne pepper

Presentation
2 tablespoons olive oil
1 cup *finely* minced onion
Mideast peta bread*

*See glossary

Using finest blade of grinder, grind lamb 3 times. Soak bulghur in water 15 minutes. Drain through several layers of cheesecloth and squeeze dry. With fingers, combine bulghur, lamb and seasonings; knead until smooth and adjust flavors to taste. Wrap and refrigerate 3 to 4 hours or longer.
Form lamb into a patty, place in center of large round serving platter and make a hollow in center for the oil. Arrange onion around patty. Just before serving surround with heated and crisped Mideast bread broken into pieces.
Makes approximately 50 buffet servings

HAM À L'ORANGE

1 10- to 12-pound ham
brown sugar
cloves
orange slices (optional)
4 tablespoons butter
1 can frozen orange juice, undiluted
1 cup ginger ale

Score ham diagonally across top and bake in 350° oven for 15 minutes. Remove from oven and pack brown sugar on top of ham, place a clove in each diagonal and top with orange slices. Return to oven for 10 minutes. Meanwhile melt butter and mix in orange juice and ginger ale. Baste ham with this mixture and continue basting every 15 minutes until the ham is cooked. Consult your butcher or the package directions for the length of cooking time. Garnish with baked pears and serve with curried kidney beans.
Makes approximately 100 buffet servings

BAKED PEARS

Fill pear halves with curry mayonnaise and sprinkle with paprika. Broil to heat. Or cut pears into wedges, drizzle mixture of honey, melted butter and mustard over wedges and broil.

buffet

ROAST BEEF PLATTER

1 10-pound bottom round of beef
1 teaspoon Sallie's Salt* or seasoned salt

Presentation
broken chicory leaves
peppermill
mushroom caps filled with pâté
bowl of horseradish or horseradish sauce
bowl of homemade mustard
100 tiny rolls

*See glossary

Have butcher cut fat off meat in one piece and tie it back on. Place in shallow roasting pan, sprinkle with salt and roast in 300° oven 20 to 30 minutes, depending upon thickness. The meat should be rare but not raw. Cool, cover and refrigerate. Discard fat and trim any remaining fat. Slice paper thin with slicer, or ask butcher to slice it.

Arrange overlapping slices of beef on large platter. Surround with chicory and sprinkle liberally with pepper. Tuck mushrooms around meat and chicory and place condiments and rolls alongside.

Makes approximately 100 buffet servings

BEEF ROLLS

Beef slices from roast beef platter can also be spread with horseradish or mustard and rolled, served either plain or on cutouts of buttered bread. (A diamond cutout, meat roll lengthwise, tiny parsley sprig on each corner.)

Cream cheese spread is also good: Combine 8 ounces cream cheese, softened, with 1 tablespoon milk, 2 tablespoons minced parsley and/or chives and seasoned salt and horseradish to taste. Spread small slices and roll. Or spread large slices of beef, roll firmly, wrap and chill. When ready to serve cut into 3/4-inch slices.

OVEN-GLAZED CORNED BEEF

3- or 4-pound piece of corned beef
water to cover
2 tablespoons pickling spices
1 small onion, cut in quarters
5 peppercorns
2 or 3 sprigs parsley
2 outside stalks celery, including leaves

Glazing Sauce
1 cup catsup
1 tablespoon dark brown sugar
1/2 teaspoon celery seed
1 tablespoon dry mustard
2 tablespoons Worcestershire sauce
2 tablespoons water

Presentation
watercress
selection of rye and pumpernickel bread
    and bagels
sweet butter
variety of hot and mild mustards
Kosher pickles, thinly sliced
horseradish
red onions, thinly sliced

Wash corned beef well in cold water. Place meat in large heavy pan and cover with water. Bring to boil and boil about 3 minutes. Pour off water and again cover with cold water. Add remaining ingredients and bring to boil. Lower heat immediately and simmer 3 to 4 hours or until meat is tender. (Or cook in a pressure cooker.) When finished, remove from water and set aside.

Combine sauce ingredients. One-half hour before serving place prepared corned beef in a shallow pan, fat side up and pour the glaze over meat. Bake in a preheated 350° oven 30 minutes.

Thinly slice meat and arrange on a large platter so slices overlap. Surround with watercress. Place choice of remaining ingredients in attractive serving dishes around meat platter.

Makes approximately 40 buffet servings

chinese buffet

CHINESE BUFFET

Deem Sum
beef sui mi
pork sui mi
fried wontons
egg rolls
guon fun
har gow
fan swa tay
baw
kuo-tieh (pot stickers)
ga lei gawk
guey biang

law pak go (turnip pudding)
parchment chicken
hem thuen jow gai (chicken in sweet
    and sour sauce)
tea eggs
sao pai gut (barbecued spareribs)
cha siew (barbecued pork)
skewered lichee nuts and kumquats

Desserts
agar-agar with water chestnuts
ahn gawk

DEEM SUM

Deem sum (little hearts) are traditionally served with tea as a light Chinese lunch. Various skins are used to encase a variety of fillings. With deem sum serve dishes of hot mustard, catsup, toasted sesame seeds and bottles of dry sherry, white vinegar, soy sauce and Aji oil*. Guests help themselves to whichever deem sum they want and use any or all of the condiments as a dip.

Wonton skins are available, square or round, in many markets and in Oriental stores. There are about 80 in a package depending upon how thin they've been rolled. If well wrapped, they may be frozen, but noodle doughs dry out quickly and become difficult to work with. Homemade skins are equally good, but without proper equipment they cannot be rolled thin enough. A noodle machine does a good job. To make your own, combine 1/2 cup hot water and 1 teaspoon each salad oil and salt. Quickly add 2 cups flour, mix well and knead until smooth. Form into 3 or 4 1/2-inch ropes, wrap each in wax paper and refrigerate 30 minutes. Working with one rope at a time, cut off 1/2-inch slices and roll as thinly as possible into squares or rounds. Stack, keeping covered, and repeat with remaining ropes. When working with finished skins, fill only a few at a time, keeping rest covered. Seal seams with a tiny bit of water and place seam side down on cookie sheet. Cover filled skins with tea towel to prevent drying out.

*See glossary

TO STEAM

Place each filled skin on a small piece of foil in bamboo steamer, place steamer over wok filled with boiling water and steam designated amount of time. If using a steamer or large kettle with rack, place in cake pan and wrap lid with towel to avoid moisture drops. Be careful water does not boil up too close to cake pan.

BEEF SUI MI

3/4 pound round wonton skins
1 pound lean ground beef
1 egg, beaten
1/4 cup minced green onion and tops
2 tablespoons soy sauce
1 tablespoon each cornstarch and sherry
1 teaspoon minced ginger root
1/2 teaspoon salt
1 1-inch piece dried tangerine peel*,
    softened and finely minced

*See glossary

Combine ingredients. Working with a few skins at a time (keep rest covered), form 1 tablespoon filling into a ball. Place in center of wonton round and bring skin up and around to cover ball completely. Steam 20 minutes. They will take on a shiny look when done.
Makes 4 dozen

chinese buffet

PORK SUI MI

3/4 pound round wonton skins
1/2 pound each ground lean pork butt and
   finely minced raw shrimp
4 dried forest mushrooms* softened
   and minced
3 tablespoons minced green onion and tops
1 tablespoon minced Chinese parsley* (optional)
1/2 cup minced water chestnuts
1 tablespoon each soy sauce and cornstarch
1 teaspoon salt
1/2 teaspoon sesame oil* (optional)
1 egg, lightly beaten
Chinese parsley garnish

*See glossary

Combine ingredients. Place 1 tablespoon on each wonton round, crimp edges of round slightly and bring up and around meat, leaving top open so meat is exposed. Place a tiny leaf of parsley in center and steam 30 minutes.
Makes 4 dozen

GUON FUN

6 sheets (14 inches in diameter) rice-flour
   noodle rounds
1 pound bean sprouts
1/2 teaspoon sesame oil*
1 tablespoon soy sauce
1 teaspoon salt
1/4 teaspoon black pepper
1/4 pound barbecued pork (page 174), slivered
1/2 cup slivered green onion
1/2 recipe egg garni*, cut into slivers
1 tablespoon toasted sesame seeds
1 tablespoon slivered pickled red ginger* (optional)
Chinese parsley sprigs* (2 to 3 per roll or to taste)

*See glossary

Rice flour noodle rounds are almost impossible to make at home. They are available in Oriental specialty shops. Skins stiffen if chilled. You may substitute crêpes and omit egg garni in recipe.
Pour boiling water over bean sprouts and let stand 1 minute. Drain, rinse in cold water and drain well. Mix with sesame oil, soy sauce, salt and pepper. Have other ingredients ready. Shortly before serving, unroll one sheet of rice-flour noodles at a time, being careful not to break. Arrange bean sprouts and rest of ingredients in order given, 1/6 at a time, on round. Roll as tightly as possible to make a cylinder about 1-1/4 inches in diameter. Repeat with remaining rounds. Serve uncooked at room temperature, garnished with extra Chinese parsley if desired, cut into 1-1/2-inch pieces.

EGG ROLLS

1 pound large square wonton skins
1 tablespoon corn oil
3 celery ribs, sliced diagonally
1 pound bean sprouts
3/4 cup slivered bamboo shoots
1 4-ounce can water chestnuts, drained
    and slivered
1 tablespoon soy sauce
1 teaspoon sugar
1/2 teaspoon sesame oil*
1/2 cup slivered green onions
1 tablespoon cornstarch
1 recipe egg garni*
Chinese parsley* (optional)

*See glossary

Heat oil and quickly cook celery, bean sprouts, bamboo shoots, water chestnuts, soy sauce and sugar 3 minutes. Pour off any juices and add sesame oil, onions, cornstarch and egg garni. Cool. Place 1/3 cup filling on lower edge of wonton skin, 1/2 inch from side edges. Fold in edges and roll like jelly roll. Seal and deep fry, seam side down, turning once, until crisp and golden. Drain on paper towels. Can be made ahead and reheated on rack in a 375° oven. To serve, cut into 1-1/2-inch pieces. If desired, when rolling add a sprig of Chinese parsley.
Makes 14 to 16 rolls

BAW

1 recipe potato bread (page 23)
2 cups finely minced cooked pork or ham
2 tablespoons minced green onion
1 tablespoon each hoisin sauce* and sherry
1 teaspoon brown bean sauce*
1 tablespoon minced Chinese parsley* (optional)
1/2 teaspoon sesame oil* (optional)
1/4 teaspoon five spices powder*
1 tablespoon corn oil
1 tablespoon cornstarch dissolved in
    1/2 cup chicken stock

*See glossary

Quickly sauté pork or ham, onion, hoisin sauce, sherry, brown bean sauce, parsley, sesame oil and five spices powder in oil to blend flavors. Add cornstarch-stock binder and cook until thickened. Cool. Follow directions for potato bread through first rising. Roll 1/4 inch thick and cut into 4-inch rounds. Put 2 tablespoons filling in center and work dough up and around to cover filling. Place seam side down on square of greased wax paper. Let rise until puffy and double in size. Bake in a 375° oven 15 minutes, or steam 20 minutes. These can be frozen and reheated after defrosting.
Makes 18

chinese buffet

FRIED WONTONS

Use any fillings from other deem sum recipes. Place
1 teaspoon filling in one corner of square wonton
skin, fold tips over into a triangle with points
off center. Press together to seal, using water if
needed, and fry in deep oil until golden. Drain on
paper toweling and serve immediately. May be
made ahead and reheated just before serving. Pass
sweet and sour sauce (page 173) for dipping as well
as other condiments mentioned in general deem
sum instructions.

GA LEI GAWK

1 recipe quick puff pastry (page 102)
1 pound lean ground beef
1/2 cup minced onion
1 teaspoon finely minced garlic
1/2 teaspoon finely minced ginger root
1 tablespoon soy sauce
1/2 teaspoon salt
1/2 to 1 teaspoon curry powder
1/4 teaspoon pepper

Combine filling ingredients and sauté lightly until
beef loses color. Cool. Roll pastry 1/8 inch thick
and cut into 3-inch rounds. Place 1 tablespoon
filling on each round, fold over into half-moon
shape and flute edges. Bake in a 375° oven 10
minutes or until golden.
Makes approximately 3 dozen

KUO-TIEH
(Pot Stickers)

3/4 pound round wonton skins
3/4 pound lean pork butt, *finely* minced
1/4 cup chopped green onion and tops
1 cup *finely* shredded Chinese cabbage
1-1/2 teaspoons minced garlic
1 teaspoon minced ginger root
1/2 teaspoon each salt and rice wine vinegar*
1/4 teaspoon pepper
1/2 teaspoon sesame oil*
6 drops Aji oil*
corn oil

*See glossary

Combine filling ingredients and adjust for seasonings. Place 1 tablespoon filling in center of skin, fold over into half-moon shape and seal edges with a little water. Cook 5 minutes in rapidly boiling water to which 1 to 2 teaspoons corn oil has been added. Drain and dry on paper toweling. Brown on one side only in a thin layer of corn oil. Serve immediately. Sprinkle with additional Aji oil, a must for this north Chinese specialty.
Makes 4 dozen

GUEY BIANG

1 pound any raw firm white fish, ground
1/2 cup each minced water chestnuts and
  chopped roasted peanuts
2 tablespoons chopped green onions
1 tablespoon chopped Chinese parsley*
1 1-inch piece dried tangerine peel*,
  softened and minced
1 tablespoon each soy sauce and sherry
2 tablespoons cornstarch
1/2 teaspoon salt
1/4 teaspoon black pepper
4 eggs, beaten with
  2 tablespoons water
1 tablespoon corn oil

*See glossary

Combine ingredients and drop by spoonfuls onto hot oiled skillet to form 3-inch cakes. Let set and over medium heat brown lightly; turn to brown other side, adding more oil as needed. Do not overcook. If making ahead undercook slightly and reheat in a moderate oven.
Makes 18 cakes

chinese buffet

HAR GOW

1 recipe wheat starch skins (following) or
    wonton skins
1 pound raw shrimp, shelled, deveined and minced
1 cup finely minced bamboo shoots
1 tablespoon each cornstarch and sherry
1/2 teaspoon each salt and sesame oil*

*See glossary

Combine ingredients. Make 4 pleats on one side of wheat starch round. Bring other side up to make a cup. Fill with 1 tablespoon of filling and bring flap up and over to make bonnet shape. Pinch to seal. Place on oiled cake pan and steam 15 minutes. Makes 4 dozen

WHEAT STARCH SKINS

2-1/2 cups wheat starch*
1 teaspoon salt
about 2 cups boiling water
corn oil

*See glossary

In bowl mix wheat starch and salt. Stirring *constantly* with chopsticks or fork, drizzle boiling water over, adding only enough to make consistency of pastry. Let stand just until cool enough to handle. Knead 10 minutes, form into ball, rub top with oil and cover with inverted bowl. Let rest 20 minutes. Form into ropes 1 inch in diameter. Pinch off 1-inch pieces and roll into a 4-inch circle. Use corn oil, not flour, to prevent sticking. Makes 4 dozen rounds

FAN SWA TAY

1 recipe wheat starch skins, preceding, or
   wonton skins

1 tablespoon corn oil
1/2 pound lean pork butt, ground
1 tablespoon minced dried preserved turnip greens*
2 tablespoons minced softened dried
   forest mushrooms*
1 1-inch piece dried tangerine peel*,
   softened and finely minced
1 tablespoon soy sauce
1/4 teaspoon salt
1/4 pound raw shrimp, shelled, deveined
   and minced
1/8 teaspoon five spices powder*
1/4 cup minced green onion and tops
1/4 teaspoon sesame oil*
1 tablespoon minced Chinese parsley* (optional)

*See glossary

Heat oil and quickly cook pork, turnip greens, mushrooms and tangerine peel until meat just loses color. Add soy, salt, shrimp, and five spices powder. Cook and stir 1 minute. Remove from heat and add onion, sesame oil and parsley. Cool. Fill, seal and cook as directed for har gow.
Makes 4 dozen

LAW PAK GO
(Turnip Pudding)

1 pound Chinese turnips*, peeled and thinly sliced
1/2 teaspoon salt
boiling water to cover
2 cups rice flour
3/4 cup cold water
1/4 cup corn oil
1/4 teaspoon salt
1 cup minced cooked ham
1 teaspoon soy sauce
2 tablespoons each chopped green onions
   and Chinese parsley*
1 tablespoon toasted sesame seeds

*See glossary

Boil turnips in salted water 10 minutes until tender. Drain and while still hot mash with flour, water, oil and salt. Add ham and soy sauce. Pour into oiled 9-inch shallow glass baking dish, cover with wax paper and steam 1-1/2 hours or until toothpick inserted in center comes out clean. Remove from steamer and immediately sprinkle with onions, Chinese parsley and sesame seeds. Serve warm or at room temperature cut in squares.
Makes 36 1-1/2-inch squares

chinese buffet

PARCHMENT CHICKEN

1 pound chicken meat, cut into small pieces
parchment paper
corn oil for deep frying

Marinade
2 tablespoons each sherry or whiskey,
    soy sauce and minced green onion
1 tablespoon each cornstarch and corn oil
1-1/2 teaspoons finely minced ginger root
1/2 teaspoon finely minced garlic
1/2 teaspoon sesame oil*
1/4 teaspoon five spices powder*

*See glossary

Combine marinade ingredients and rub into chicken. Marinate at room temperature 2 hours. Cut parchment paper, double wax paper or butcher's paper into 24 6-inch squares. Divide filling on squares. To encase, follow directions below. Deep fry in hot oil 2 minutes per side. Drain on paper toweling and serve on shredded lettuce. May be made ahead and reheated 10 to 15 minutes on rack in a 375° oven.
Makes 24

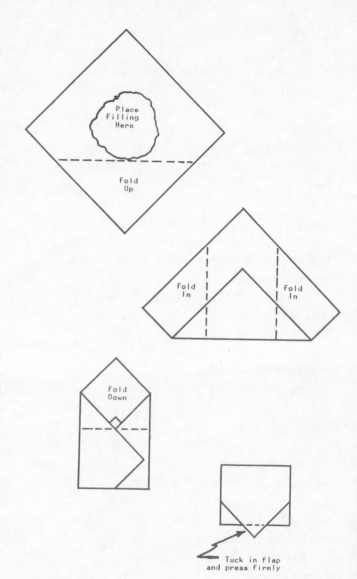

HEM THUEN JOW GAI
(Chicken in Sweet and Sour Sauce)

1-1/2 pounds chicken meat cut into 1-inch
    cubes (or chicken wings, cut at joints)
preceding parchment chicken marinade with
    3 tablespoons green onions added
1 egg, beaten
1/2 cup flour
corn oil for deep frying

Presentation
shredded lettuce
1/4 cup toasted sesame seeds
preserved mixed vegetable relish*

*See glossary

Marinate chicken 1 hour. Place in bowl with egg
and stir to coat well. Add flour and coat. Deep fry
in 1/2 inch hot oil until golden (do not crowd).
Drain on paper toweling. Toss chicken in sweet and
sour sauce and arrange on shredded lettuce. Sprinkle with sesame seeds and serve hot or at room
temperature with preserved mixed vegetable relish
on the side.
Makes approximately 12 servings
depending upon other dishes being served

SWEET AND SOUR SAUCE

1 cup cold water
2 tablespoons each catsup, vinegar,
    cornstarch and sugar
1-1/2 tablespoons plum sauce* (optional)

*See glossary

Combine ingredients and heat until slightly thickened. Adjust to taste.

SAO PAI GUT
(Barbecued Spareribs)

1/4 cup each hoisin sauce* and sugar
1 tablespoon each oyster sauce* and sherry
1/4 teaspoon five spices powder*
1/4 teaspoon saltpeter (optional)
2-1/2 pounds *lean* spareribs, halved
    lengthwise and cracked

*See glossary

Combine marinade ingredients and rub well into
spareribs. Marinate at room temperature 4 hours.
Bake in a 375° oven 40 minutes.

chinese buffet

CHA SIEW
(Barbecued Pork)

2 pounds lean pork butt strips (1-1/2 inches thick)

Marinate as for preceding spareribs. Bake on rack 45 minutes. Cool slightly before serving. Slice thinly on the diagonal.

TEA EGGS

1 cup strong black tea
3/4 cup vinegar
1 tablespoon sugar
1/2 teaspoon salt
3 slices ginger root
12 *small* hard-cooked eggs, shelled

Bring tea, vinegar, sugar, salt and ginger root to boil. Cool. Place eggs in jar, pour tea mixture over, cover and refrigerate 2 to 6 days. Cut into halves.
Makes 24

AHN GAWK

1 cup milk or diluted evaporated milk
2 eggs, beaten
2-1/2 tablespoons sugar
1 teaspoon almond extract
24 prebaked small tart shells from
    short crust pastry (page 102)

Combine milk, eggs, sugar and almond extract. Sieve and pour into shells. Bake in a 375° oven 15 minutes or until toothpick inserted in center of custard comes out clean. Remove from tins and cool on rack.
Makes 2 dozen

AGAR-AGAR WITH WATER CHESTNUTS

1/2 cup sugar
3 cups water
1 stick kanten*, cut up
1 teaspoon almond extract
1/2 cup finely minced water chestnuts

*See glossary

Dissolve sugar in water. Add kanten and soak 5 minutes. Bring just to boil and simmer 10 minutes. Add extract and water chestnuts. Pour into shallow dish, cool and refrigerate to set. Cut into squares and place on serving plate.
Makes approximately 20 servings

GYPSY TABLE

Choice of
assorted cold cuts
chicken marinated in mint marinade
   (Mideast, page 143) and barbecued
beef roasted with salt, pepper and rosemary,
   then thinly sliced
pork roasted with anise
goose roasted with sage and marjoram
roast pig (recipe follows)

bokoli (recipe follows)
pieces of feta or any goat cheese
small ripe salty Greek olives
meatballs rolled in nutmeg (recipe follows)
sautéed eggplant chunks served
   at room temperature
black bread

bowls of
yoghurt
toasted sesame seeds
sliced cucumbers
sliced tomatoes
cooked white beans and chopped pimiento
   dressed with vinegar
chickpeas in tahini
cooked green beans dressed with sour cream
lentils cooked with diced onion, allspice,
   salt and pepper, and dressed with lemon juice
   and grated orange peel

buffet

ROAST PIG

1 pig
olive oil
garlic cloves, quartered
rosemary sprigs
salt and pepper

In specialty markets a small dressed suckling pig may cost as much as a 50-pound baby pig, so size depends upon number of guests, other dishes to be served and charcoal spit equipment at hand or rentable (2 to 5 feet).

The night before, rub inside of suckling pig generously with olive oil and tuck in garlic cloves and rosemary. Sprinkle inside and out with salt and pepper. If pig is over 20 pounds, cut deeply in crisscross pattern inside thighs and slit between ribs without breaking outer skin. Rub cavity and cuts with oil and tuck garlic cloves and rosemary sprigs into cavity and cuts. Sprinkle inside and out with salt and pepper. Close cavity and tie loosely; keep refrigerated or in cool place overnight.

Since a cleaned pig is slit, spitting is more critical than with a fowl. Secure spit tightly against the backbone, preferably with wire at several spots to keep pig from flapping as it turns. Forked skewers at either end of the spit should be forced toward the center before being tightened. Tie legs along spit with heavy twine or wire in parallel position; wrap torso tightly with several loops of twine or wire to close cavity. Secure ears over face with skewers.

Roast 6 to 12 inches from deep, vigorously glowing bed of charcoal from 3 to 6 hours depending on size of pig and area of coals. If drippings flame and char the skin prematurely, clear a channel under dripping area. Add charcoal frequently along periphery of fire. Prick skin after 1 hour.

The entire surface of the pig should eventually look charred. If done before ready to serve, fire can be cooled down or spit raised.

To serve: Transfer to large platter or board and carve. Larger pigs can be severed at midsection while still on the skewer and then removed.

BOKOLI

1 recipe pannequets (page 131)
1/2 pound ground lean lamb
2 tablespoons finely minced onion
1/2 teaspoon minced garlic
1/2 teaspoon salt
1/4 teaspoon pepper
1/8 teaspoon cumin
2 tablespoons each minced parsley and mint
1 to 2 tablespoons pine nuts
2 tablespoons tomato purée
1/4 cup chopped cooked spinach (optional)

Sauté lamb, onion and garlic 3 minutes until lamb loses color. Do not brown. Add seasonings, parsley, mint, pine nuts, tomato purée and optional spinach. Adjust seasonings to taste and cool. Fill pannequets and place seam side down in chafing dish. Heat before serving.

BEEF BALLS ROLLED IN NUTMEG

1 cup chopped onion
1 egg
2 tablespoons cold water
1/2 cup fine bread crumbs
1 teaspoon salt
1/4 teaspoon each pepper and cumin
1 pound ground chuck
very fine bread crumbs
oil for deep frying
nutmeg

In blender purée onion, egg and water. Combine with crumbs, seasonings and ground meat. Sauté a small amount and adjust seasonings to taste. Form into balls approximately 1 inch in diameter, roll lightly in fine bread crumbs and chill 1 hour. Deep fry until golden, about 1 minute, and drain on paper toweling. While hot roll in nutmeg to taste. Serve hot or at room temperature.
Makes approximately 4 dozen

OTHER BUFFET SUGGESTIONS

• In shallow crystal bowl layer 8 ounces cream cheese softened with 2 tablespoons mayonnaise, 1 3-3/4-ounce jar lumpfish caviar, 1/2 cup minced green onions and tops and 2 hard-cooked eggs, sieved. Sprinkle with paprika and grated lemon peel. Serve with plain crackers or melba toast.

• Peel and thinly slice jicama. Cut into bite-sized pieces and marinate several hours in lime juice. Serve in crystal bowl with sprinkling of salt and chili powder or cayenne pepper.

• With canape cutters cut shapes from cheese and bologna sliced 1/4 inch thick. Thread 1 of each on small bamboo skewer.

• Soften cream cheese with cream and place in center of large round platter. Sprinkle with paprika. Arrange an assortment of smoked oysters, clams and/or octopus around and tuck sprigs of parsley in for color. Surround with an assortment of crackers.

• Bowl of marinated artichoke hearts, chopped green onions, minced parsley, cherry tomatoes.

• Arrange tiny chilled cooked or canned carrots on bed of mint leaves and sprinkle with finely minced parsley.

• Arrange cooked marinated Brussels sprouts on serving platter and sprinkle with dill weed.

• Combine and heat 3/4 cup prepared mustard and 1 10-ounce jar currant jelly. Add 2 to 2-1/2 pounds cooked cocktail sausages and reheat. Serve in chafing dish.

• On wooden board attractively arrange thinly sliced lox, thinly sliced black bread, capers, minced onions and cornichons.

• Dress sliced cooked cervalet sausage, slices of garlic, and green onion bulbs sliced lengthwise with oil and vinegar.

buffet desserts

COOKIE BOWS

1 tablespoon lard
2 teaspoons sugar
1/8 teaspoon salt
2 egg yolks
1/2 cup unbleached flour
powdered sugar

Cream lard, sugar and salt. Beat in yolks one at a time. Add flour, blend and turn out onto floured board. Knead 10 minutes, using only enough flour to make smooth, elastic dough. Cover with tea towel and let rest 20 minutes. Roll as thinly as possible and cut into 1x2-inch rectangles. Slit from opposite ends the long way into stylized block "S." Pick up ends of "S" and carefully tie loose overhand knot. Fry in deep oil until golden on both sides, turning once. Drain on paper toweling, sprinkle with powdered sugar while hot and again when cool.
Makes 4 to 5 dozen

ROQUEFORT COOKIES

2-1/4 cups sifted flour
1/2 cup sifted powdered sugar
1/2 teaspoon salt
1/2 teaspoon white pepper
1/2 pound butter
1 cup crumbled Roquefort cheese
3 tablespoons dry sherry
1-2/3 cups finely chopped toasted walnuts

Sift flour with sugar, salt and pepper; cut in butter to make very fine particles. Add cheese and mix well with a wooden spoon. Sprinkle sherry and 1 cup chopped walnuts over mixture and mix to a stiff dough. Shape dough into two rolls, about 9 inches long. Roll in remaining 2/3 cup of chopped walnuts, pressing walnuts firmly into the dough. Wrap in wax paper and chill thoroughly. When ready to serve, cut into 1/4-inch slices. Place on lightly greased cookie sheets and bake in a 400° oven about 8 minutes or until lightly browned. Cool on wire cake racks. Serve with fruit and cheese.
Makes about 60 cookies

APRICOT BALLS

1-1/2 cups dried apricots, ground or finely chopped
2 cups shredded coconut
2/3 cup sweetened condensed milk
1/2 cup ground almonds or walnuts
powdered sugar

Place all ingredients except powdered sugar into a large mixing bowl; mix well. Form into small balls and roll in powdered sugar. Let stand 1 hour and again roll in powdered sugar. Can be served at this point or stored in an airtight container. May be frozen. For variation, use toasted coconut.
Makes 3 dozen balls

BUFFET STRAWBERRIES

Purchase large long-stemmed strawberries if possible and leave stems on. Wash, dry and mound attractively on serving platter. Surround with sprigs of mint and several dishes of dips.
• Sour cream and brown sugar in separate bowls.
• Mixture of sour cream and powdered sugar and Cointreau to taste.
• Cream cheese softened to dipping consistency with sour cream and sprinkled with brown sugar and cinnamon (room temperature).
• Mixture of sour cream and powdered sugar, lemon juice, grated lemon peel and orange-flavored liqueur to taste.

buffet desserts

CANNOLI

6 cannoli tubes (or cut 1-inch-in-diameter
  aluminum tubing or wooden dowels into
  6-inch lengths)
4 dozen wonton skins (page 165)**

Place tubes diagonally across center of squares and
wrap skins around, sealing tips with water. Lower a
few at a time into deep hot vegetable oil seam side
down; fry 30 seconds or until just golden. Remove
and drain on paper toweling; while still hot gently
push off tube. Cool before storing in airtight container. May be made in advance or may be frozen.

**Wonton skins are almost identical to basic cannoli
  dough. If making your own wonton skins, substitute wine for the water.

Filling

2 pounds ricotta cheese, beaten until
  smooth or sieved
1 cup powdered sugar, or to taste
2 teaspoons vanilla
2/3 cup shaved semi-sweet chocolate
2 to 3 minced glacé cherries or citron (optional)
ground pistachio nuts
powdered sugar
sprigs of mint for garnish

Combine cheese, 1 cup powdered sugar, vanilla and
chocolate. Cover and chill. Just before serving fill
cannoli shells. Dip ends in pistachio nuts and sprinkle cannoli with powdered sugar. Garnish serving
plate with mint.
Makes 4 dozen

Filling variation
• Omit vanilla and add liqueur or rum to taste.
Sprinkle with powdered sugar mixed with instant
espresso or dark cocoa; substitute candied orange
peel for cherries or citron.

DESSERT FONDUE

6 ounces semi-sweet chocolate chips
1/4 cup heavy cream
4 ounces sweet chocolate broken into pieces
2 tablespoons Kirsch, Cointreau or
    brandy (optional)

To be Dipped (one or all)
fresh strawberries
banana chunks
pineapple chunks
drained maraschino cherries
apple wedges
cubes of angel food cake
lady fingers
cubes of pound cake
marshmallows

small bowls of chopped walnuts and
    coconut flakes

Heat chocolate chips in cream over low heat or in a double boiler until partially melted. Add sweet chocolate and stir until melted. Add liqueur, if desired. Remove from heat and transfer to fondue pot or chafing dish to keep warm.
Guests dip selection into chocolate mixture then into nuts or coconut.
Serves 6

FONDUE VARIATIONS

• *White Fondue* Follow directions for chocolate fondue substituting 10 ounces white chocolate for the chocolate chips and sweet chocolate. White crème de menthe or crème de noyeaux may be added for additional flavor.
• *Orange Cream Fondue* Combine 2 tablespoons powdered sugar, 1 tablespoon fresh orange juice, 1 teaspoon grated fresh orange peel, 1/8 teaspoon salt and 1/2 pint sour cream. Chill before serving.
• *Honey-Spice Fondue* Combine 3 ounces cream cheese, 1/4 cup honey, 1/2 cup sour cream and 1/4 teaspoon allspice or cinnamon. Chill before serving.
• *Fruit Fondue* Combine 1/2 cup heavy cream, whipped, 4 teaspoons ground sweet chocolate, 1-1/2 teaspoons powdered sugar and 2 tablespoons undiluted frozen orange juice, thawed. Chill before serving.
• *Dessert Cheese Fondue* Combine and melt 8 ounces each cream cheese and Teleme cheese and 1/2 cup dry white wine. Transfer to chafing dish and season to taste with nutmeg.

buffet desserts

KRUM KAKES

1/4 pound butter
1 cup sugar
2 eggs
1 cup milk
1-1/4 cups flour
1 teaspoon vanilla extract or
    1/2 teaspoon almond extract

Cream butter and sugar, beat in eggs one at a time and alternately add milk and flour. Add vanilla or almond extract.

Heat krum kake iron, brush with oil and pour about 1 tablespoon batter in center of iron. Close iron and press gently. Cook 45 seconds and flip iron over. Cook another 45 seconds. The first kake may require a little longer cooking time until heat can be regulated. Kakes should be dark golden in color but not brown. Remove kake with spatula and immediately roll around a cone mold, a cannoli tube or the outside of a small cup. Cool and store or freeze in airtight container. Just before serving, place cones or tubes in a glass, fill and garnish. Serve cones upright in a bowl of sugar, tubes on a plate.

Filling: Whipped cream, sweetened (optional); top with marmalade and shaved chocolate or crushed hard candies. See also fillings for cannoli.

Cups: Dip edges of cups in melted chocolate and then in powdered sugar; fill with ice cream.

Wafers: Do not form, but leave cookies as they are just after removing from iron. Serve as a cookie or as a doily for a scoop of ice cream.

RUSSIAN WALNUT TORTE

12 eggs, separated
2 cups sugar
1 cup fine bread crumbs
1 to 1-1/2 tablespoons freshly grated lemon rind
1 pound shelled walnuts, ground
1 teaspoon cream of tartar

Beat egg yolks, add sugar and beat until smooth. Stir in bread crumbs, lemon rind and all but 1/4 cup walnuts. Beat egg whites until frothy, add cream of tartar and beat until very stiff. Fold 1/3 of walnut mixture into beaten whites. Then carefully fold in remaining walnut mixture. Line a 9-inch spring-form pan with foil, bringing sides up 3 inches. Pour torte mixture in and bake in a 350° oven 1 hour or until toothpick inserted in center comes out clean. Cool on rack 10 minutes, turn out and cool on rack.

Filling
1/2 pound sweet butter, softened
1-2/3 cups powdered sugar
4 egg yolks
1/4 cup hot *strong* coffee or cocoa

Cream butter, sugar and egg yolks. Gradually pour in *hot* coffee or cocoa. Let cool slightly. Cut torte into 4 layers. Frost and stack layers, frost top and sprinkle with reserved ground walnuts.
Serves 16 to 20

PHYLLO DESSERT TRIANGLES
(Trigona)

1 package phyllo dough (page 112)
melted butter

Syrup
1/2 cup water
3/4 cup sugar
2 tablespoons honey
1 tablespoon lemon or lime juice
1/2 teaspoon cinnamon

Filling
1 cup each walnut meats and blanched almonds
6 tablespoons sugar
2 egg yolks
3 tablespoons brandy
1/2 teaspoon each vanilla, allspice and cinnamon
1 teaspoon freshly grated lemon peel

Combine water, sugar, honey, lemon or lime juice and cinnamon. Bring to boil and stir to dissolve sugar. Simmer 10 minutes and set aside. Grind nuts and combine with rest of ingredients. Brush 1 sheet of phyllo at a time with melted butter and cut into 8 widthwise strips. Place 1/2 tablespoon filling on bottom, fold dough over to make triangle and keep folding flag style. Brush lavishly with melted butter and bake in a 375° oven 15 minutes or until golden. Cool slightly, prick all over with tines of fork and pour syrup over. Serve hot or room temperature.
Makes approximately 4-1/2 dozen

buffet desserts

SUGGESTIONS FOR DESSERT CHEESE TRAYS FOR 12
(2 pounds cheese)

- *Cheese Tray I*
Triple crème or Gormandise with Kirsch
Banon
Camembert
Bresse (blue)

- *Cheese Tray II*
Brie
Montrachet
Boursalt or La Bouille
Reblochon

- *Serve with*
French bread or bland crackers
Fruit such as apples, peaches, pears, apricots

OTHER DESSERT SUGGESTIONS

- Soften and combine 1 pint each vanilla ice cream and orange sherbert. Fold in 1/2 cup heavy cream, whipped, and 1/3 cup ground filberts. Pack into pots de crème and refreeze. Just before serving top with chilled orange marmalade and whipped cream.
- Combine 1/2 gallon slightly softened vanilla ice cream, 1 ounce cognac and 2 ounces Tia Maria. Refreeze in individual dishes.
- Marinate papaya, mango and pineapple cubes and lichee nuts in Japanese plum wine several hours. Serve with cocktail picks.
- Marinate pears in Kirsch, top with raspberry sauce and sprinkle with grated chocolate.
- Marinate honeydew melon balls in bourbon 2 to 3 hours.
- Marinate pineapple chunks in white wine. Garnish with strawberries.
- Add 2 tablespoons sugar to chou batter. Fill baked choux with sweetened whipped cream flavored with instant coffee powder or vanilla or almond extract.
- Marinate strawberries in concentrated frozen orange juice and Grand Marnier. Just before serving sprinkle with powdered sugar.

glossary
and
index

glossary

AJI OIL A chili oil made of sesame oil and cayenne pepper. Available in Oriental markets.*

BEAN CURD, FIRM Bean cakes made of puréed soybeans. Also called tofu. Available in Oriental markets and some supermarkets.*

BEAN THREAD NOODLES Opaque white noodles made from ground mung beans. Sold by weight in coiled bundles. Also called cellophane, peastarch and transparent noodles. Available in Oriental markets.*

BROWN BEAN SAUCE Thick sauce of fermented yellow beans, flour and salt. Sold in one pound or more cans in Chinese markets.*

CHINESE PARSLEY In Latin American countries called cilantro or culantro; in Middle and Far Eastern countries called coriander. An herb with fan-shaped leaves and a slightly pungent flavor.

CHINESE TURNIPS A long white radish of delicate flavor. Available in Oriental markets.

CILANTRO See Chinese parsley.

CLARIFIED BUTTER Put butter in cup and let stand over hot water until milky sediment separates and goes to bottom. Pour through a sieve lined with cheesecloth which has been wrung out in cold water, leaving milky sediment in cup.

CORIANDER See Chinese parsley.

DAIKON Japanese white radish. Available in Oriental markets.

DASHI Basic Japanese broth made of water, dried bonito flakes and seaweed. Available in instant form at Japanese markets.*

EGG GARNI Beat 4 eggs with 2 tablespoons water and 1/2 teaspoon salt. Heat 1 tablespoon corn oil in a heavy skillet, pour in half the egg mixture and cook over medium heat until set. Turn out on cutting board and repeat with rest of egg mixture. Cool, roll and slice thinly. If using as a wrapper, cook in smaller pan (6 to 8 inches) and do not roll and cut.

FIVE SPICES POWDER A spice blend of cinnamon, ginger, fennel, sugar and star anise. Sold in Oriental markets.*

FOREST MUSHROOMS, DRIED Dried black mushrooms sold by weight in Oriental markets.*

GARLIC OLIVE OIL To 1 pint olive oil add 2 bruised garlic cloves. Let stand 2 days or up to 2 weeks before changing garlic.

HOISIN SAUCE A thick dark sauce of soybeans, garlic, chili and spices. Available in Oriental markets.*

ITALIAN PARSLEY Broad-leafed parsley easily grown from seed. Has a more concentrated flavor than curly-leafed variety.

KANTEN Used as a thickening agent for Oriental desserts. Also called agar-agar, shirokaku (white) or akakaku (red). Sold by weight in Oriental markets.*

KATSUOBUSHI Fish flakes sold by weight in Oriental markets.* Also called bonito flakes.

KIM CHEE Korean relish of fermented Chinese cabbage, ginger root, garlic, green onion and hot chili pepper. Available in Oriental and other markets.

KOMBU Dried sheet kelp. Available in Japanese markets.*

LEMON DILL, LEMON LUAU Lemon seasonings adding distinctive flavor. Can be found in specialty shops, gourmet sections of department stores and delicatessens. If unable to obtain, write Shoffeitt Products Corp., Healdsburg, California 95448.

LOP CHIANG Chinese sweet pork sausage sold in Oriental markets.

MATSUBA Large Japanese herb easily grown from seed.

MEXICAN-STYLE HOT LEMON SEASONING See Lemon Dill.

MIDEAST PETA BREAD Mideast bread sold packaged in some markets or in Mideast specialty shops. Also sold frozen under the name Sahara Bread. If unable to find, write Sahara Baking Co., Inc., 349 Lincoln Street, Hingham, Massachusetts 02043.

MIRIN A sweet Japanese cooking wine available in Oriental markets and some supermarkets. May substitute sherry with a little sugar.

MISO, WHITE Sold as shirumiso in Oriental markets. A fermented paste of malt, soybeans and salt.*

NORI Sheet seaweed available in Oriental markets.*

OYSTER SAUCE Thick oyster-flavored sauce available in Oriental markets and some supermarkets.*

PHYLLO DOUGH Paper-thin pastry dough available in Middle Eastern shops. See page 112.

PICKLED RED GINGER Also called yosaburo zuke. Ginger pickled in vinegar brine. Sold in Oriental markets.*

PLUM SAUCE Thick sauce made from plums, chili and spices. Available in Oriental markets.*

PRESERVED MIXED VEGETABLE RELISH Sweet shredded cucumber and carrot. Sold in cans at Oriental markets.*

PRESERVED TURNIP GREENS Also called choong toy. Turnips and their tops preserved with salt, dried and rolled. Sold in Oriental markets.*

RICE VINEGAR Mild vinegar available in Oriental markets.*

SALLIE'S SALT Special salt and pepper mixture. If unable to find, write Emprise, 619 Barbera Place, Davis, California 95616.

SESAME OIL Strong in flavor; more an extract than an oil. Sold in Oriental markets and some supermarkets.*

SESAME SEED PASTE A seasoned sesame paste made from soya bean paste, sesame and sugar.

TANGERINE PEEL, DRIED Dried tangerine, mandarin orange or orange peel. Sold by weight in Oriental stores.*

WASABI Green horseradish powder available in Japanese markets.* Mix with just enough cold water to make a paste. Let stand 15 minutes.

WHEAT STARCH Wheat flour with gluten removed. Sold in one-pound sacks in Chinese markets.

*If unable to obtain, write P.O. Box 1074, San Rafael, California 94901 for mail-order price list.

index

Abalone Balls, 122
Agar-Agar with Water Chestnuts, 174
Ahn Gawk, 174
Almond-Chicken Balls, 60
Anchovy Sauce, 10
Antipasto, 50
Antipasto Rounds, 49
Appetizers, Cold, 46 (See also, Balls)
   Antipasto, 50
   Antipasto Rounds, 49
   Artichoke Bottoms, Filled, 56
   Beets, Filled, 53
   Celery, Stuffed, 52
   Cheese Roll-ups, 47
   Cherry Tomatoes, Stuffed, 53
   Dolmas, 57
   Eggs, Stuffed, 54-55
   Lox Roll-ups, 48
   Mushrooms, Filled Raw, 54
   Roll-ups, 47
   Sashimi, 51
   Shrimp Bowl, 49
   Shrimp, Stuffed, 52
   Sushi, 58-59
Appetizers, Hot, 62
   Cheese Balls, Deep-Fried, 64
   Crescent Roll, 66
   Mushrooms, Hot Stuffed, 63
   Rumaki, 62
   Shrimp, Broiled Marinated, 64
   Shrimp Triangles, Deep-Fried, 65
   Toast Cups, 66
Apple Butter Soup, 91
Apricot Balls, 179
Artichoke Bottoms, Filled, 56
Asparagus Quiche, 117
Aspic Canapes, 40
Aspic, Coating with, 18
Aspic Cutouts, 18

Aspic, Decorating Foods
   Coated with, 17-18
Aspic Jellies
   Consommé, 17
   Madeira, 17
   Madrilene, 17
   Mayonnaise Collée, 17
   Stocks, 17
   Tomato, 17
   Vegetable, 17
Aspic, Lining Containers with, 17
Avocado Butter, 28
Avocado Mold, 71
Avocado Ring with Fruit, 150

Bagna Cauda Fondue, 140
Balls
   Almond-Chicken, 60
   Cheddar-Chili, 61
   Cheddar-Olive, 61
   Cheese, Deep-Fried, 64
   Chutney-Chicken, 60
   Clam-Veal, 60
   Gorgonzola, 60
   Ham and Egg, 61
   Shrimp, 61
Balls for Chafing Dish
   Abalone, 122
   Chicken/Turkey Balls in Wine
     Sauce, 124
   Lamb Meatballs, 126
   Lamb Meatballs, Minted, 126
   Polpotte, 123
   Pork-Clam, 123
   Sauerkraut, 124
   Shrimp, Deep-Fried, 122
   Sweet-Sour Meatballs, 125
Barbecue, 142, 144-145
Barbecued Pork (Cha Siew), 174
Barbecued Spareribs (Sao Pai But), 173

Baw, 167
Béarnaise Sauce, 7
Beef Balls Rolled in Nutmeg, 177
Beef Empanaditas, 110
Beef Fondue, 139
Beef Piroshki, 111
Beef Platter, 162
Beef Rolls, 162
Beef Sui Mi, 165
Beets, Filled, 53
Blue Cheese Mold, 74
Boiled or Cream Dressing, 11
Bokoli, 176
Boning Fowl, 81
Bordelaise Sauce, 9
Böreks, 115
Bouchées, 103
Braunschweiger-Cream Cheese Mold, 73
Bread Ideas, Quick, 44
Breads
   Brown, 22
   Cheese Cutouts, 26
   Chive, 24
   Cornucopias, 25
   Croûtes, 25
   Egg, 23
   Melba Toasts, 26
   Potato, 23
   Pumpkin, 25
   Whole Wheat/Rye, 24
Brown Bread, 22
Buffet Hints, 147
Buffet Suggestions, 177
Butters, Seasoned, 27

Canapes, Cold, 37-39
   Aspic, 40
   Chicken Roll, 40

index

Canapes, Hot, 41, 44
  Crab, 42
  Gorgonzola, 43
  Mushroom, 42
  Quick Bread Ideas, 44
  Tomato-Cheese Rounds, 43
Cannoli, 180
Caviar Mold, 72
Celeriac Salad, 150
Celery Seed Dip, 69
Celery, Stuffed, 52
Chafing Dish Suggestions, Easy, 131
Cha Siew (Barbecued Pork), 174
Cheddar Cheese Pastry, 101
Cheddar-Chili Balls, 61
Cheddar-Olive Balls, 61
Cheese Balls, Deep-Fried, 64
Cheese-Beer Soup, 91
Cheese Custard Molds, 94
Cheese Cutouts, 26
Cheese Fondue, 138
Cheese Pastry, Quick, 101
Cheese Quiche, 116
Cheese Roll-ups, 47
Cheese Pasties, 107
Cheese Tray for Buffet, 151
Cheese Tray for Dessert, 184
Cherry Tomatoes, Stuffed, 53
Chicken Dip, 69
Chicken-Cheese Filling for Phyllo, 113
Chicken Cheese Fondue, 140
Chicken Galantine, 84
Chicken in Sweet and Sour Sauce
  (Hem Thuen Jow Gai), 173
Chicken Liver Mousse, 74
Chicken Liver Pâté, 74
Chicken Liver Pâté, Baked, 75
Chicken Liver Pâté, Spicy Baked, 75
Chicken Livers and Gizzards, 130
Chicken Mousse, 93

Chicken Piroshki, 111
Chicken Roll Canapes, 40
Chicken/Turkey Balls in Wine Sauce, 124
Chicken Wings, 157
Chili Empanaditas, 110
Chinese Buffet (Deem Sum), 164-174
Chinese Firepot, 135
Chive Bread, 24
Choux, 108-109
Chutney-Chicken Balls, 60
Chutney Sauce, 9
Clam Dip, 68
Clam-Veal Balls, 60
Clarifying Stock, 13
Consommé Jelly, 17
Cookie Bows, 178
Corned Beef, Oven-Glazed, 163
Cornucopias, 25
Cottage Cheese Pastry, 101
Cottage Cheese Spread, 30
Crab and Shrimp Mousse, 159
Crab Canapes, 42
Crab Filling for Phyllo, 114
Crab Melba, 128
Crab Quiche, 119
Cream Cheese Pastry, 101
Crescent Roll Appetizers, 66
Croustades, 120
Croûtes, 25
Cucumber Dip, 67
Cucumber Soup, 89
Curry Sauce, 8

Deem Sum, see Chinese Buffet
Desserts for Buffet
  Apricot Balls, 179
  Cannoli, 180
  Cookie Bows, 178
  Cheese Tray, 184
  Dessert Suggestions, 184

  Fondues, 181
  Krum Kakes, 182
  Phyllo Dessert Triangles (Trigona), 183
  Roquefort Cookies, 178
  Russian Walnut Torte, 183
  Strawberries, 179
Dips, 67
  Celery Seed, 69
  Chicken, 69
  Clam Dip, 68
  Cucumber, 67
  Guacamole, 69
  Peppercorn, 68
  Spinach, 67
  Zucchini, 68
Dolmas, 57
Dressings, see Sauces and Dressings

Egg-Aspic Cutouts, 18
Egg Bread, 23
Egg Rolls, 167
Eggplant Rolls, 98
Eggplant Spread, 28
Eggs, Poached, in Aspic, 92
Eggs, Stuffed, 54-55
Eggs with Tepenade Sauce, 155
Empanaditas, 110
  Beef, 110
  Chili, 110

Fan Swa Tay, 171
Fans for Garnishing, 16
Feta Cheese Filling for Phyllo
  (Tiropetes), 114
Filled Garnitures, 16
Fillings and Spreads, 32-33

index

Firepots, Oriental, 134
  Chinese, 135
  Korean Sin Sul Lo, 137
  Japanese Mizutaki, 136
  Mongolian, 134
Fish Stock, 13
Fondues, 138
  Bagna Cauda, 140
  Beef, 139
  Cheese, 138
  Chicken Cheese, 140
  Lamb, 139
Fondues, Dessert, 181
French Dressing, 11

Galantines, 81
  Chicken, 84
  Turkey, 82-83
  Veal, 85
Ga Lei Gawk, 168
Game Stock, 13
Garnitures, 14, 19
  Aspic Cutouts, 18
  Egg-Aspic Cutouts, 18
  Fans, 16
  Filled, 16
  Lemons, Oranges and Limes, 16
  Vegetable Flowers, 14
Gorgonzola Balls, 60
Gorgonzola Canapes, 43
Green Tomato Quiche, 117
Guacamole, 69
Guey Biang, 169
Guon Fun, 166
Gypsy Table, 175-177

Ham à l'Orange, 161
Ham and Egg Balls, 61
Ham and Parsley in Aspic, 153
Har Gow, 170

Hem Thuen Jow Gai (Chicken in Sweet
  and Sour Sauce), 173
Herb Sauce, 9
Herb Soup, Chilled, 90
Herring, Pickled, 152
Hints, General Cooking, 20
Hollandaise Sauce, 7
Horseradish Sauce, 10
Horseradish Mold, 73

Japanese Mizutaki, 136
Jellies, see Aspic Jellies

Kibbee, 161
Kidney Beans, Curried, 154
Korean Sin Sul Lo, 137
Krum Kakes, 182
Kuo-Tieh (Pot Stickers), 169

Lamb Fondue, 139
Lamb Kidneys in Madeira Sauce, 128
Lamb Meatballs, 126
Lamb Meatballs, Minted, 126
Law Pak Go (Turnip Pudding), 171
Lemon Curd, 30
Lemons, Oranges, and Limes for
  Garnishing, 16
Lettuce Soup, 87
Liver Pâté, Mock, 77
Lobster-Mushroom Coquilles, 97
Lox Roll-ups, 48

Madeira Jelly, 17
Madrilene Jelly, 17
Marinades, 142
  Game and Poultry, 143
  Ham, 144
  Lamb, Beef and their Innards, 143
  Oriental, 144
  Pork, 144
  Seafood, 142

Marinated Vegetables, 148
Mayonnaise Collée, 17
Mayonnaises, 6
Meat Stock, 13
Melba Toasts, 26
Mizutaki, Japanese, 136
Mock Liver Pâté, 77
Molds, 71
  Avocado, 71
  Avocado Ring with Fruit, 150
  Blue Cheese, 72
  Braunschweiger-Cream Cheese, 73
  Caviar, 72
  Cheese Custard, 94
  Horseradish, 73
  Tomato Custard, 94
  Watercress Cream, 149
Mongolian Firepot, 134
Mornay Sauce, 8
Mousseline Sauce, 8
Mousses, Plain
  Chicken, 93
  Chicken Liver, 74
  Crab and Shrimp, 159
  Tuna, 159
Mushroom Canapes, 42
Mushroom Duxelle, 12
Mushroom Pasties, 107
Mushroom Quiche, 118
Mushrooms, Filled Raw, 54
Mushrooms, Hot Stuffed, 63

Omelet Pancakes, 141
Onion Pie (Zwielbelkuchen), 154
Orange Dressing, 150
Oriental Firepots, 134-137

Pannequets, 131
Parchment Chicken, 172

index

Pasties, 106
  Cheese, 106
  Mushroom, 107
  Shrimp, 107
Pastry Balls, 106
Pastry Dough, 101
  Cheddar Cheese, 101
  Cheese, Quick, 101
  Cottage Cheese, 101
  Cream Cheese, 101
  Pastry for Casing, 78
  Phyllo, 112
  Pizza, 103
  Puff, Quick, 102
  Short Crust, 102
  Sour Cream, 102
Pastry Fingers, Puff, 105
Pastry Rolls, Pork, 104
Pastry Squares, Puff, 105
Pâté en Croûte, 78-79
Pâtés
  Chicken Liver, 74
  Chicken Liver, Baked, 75
  Chicken Liver, Spicy Baked, 75
  Mock Liver, 77
  Pâté en Croûte, 78-79
  Pork, 76
  Tuna, 76
Pea Soup, 90
Pears, Baked, 161
Peppercorn Dip, 68
Peta Sandwiches, 35
Phyllo Dessert Triangles (Trigona), 183
Phyllo Dough, 112
Phyllo Pastry Fillings
  Chicken-Cheese, 113
  Crab, 114
  Dessert Triangles (Trigona), 183
  Feta Cheese (Tiropetes), 114
  Spinach, 113
  Veal, 115

Phyllo Rolls, 112
Phyllo Triangles, 112
Pickled Herring, 152
Pickled Vegetables, 148
Pig, Roast, 176
Pinwheel Sandwiches, 34
Piroshki, 110
  Beef, 111
  Chicken, 111
Pissaladière, 156
Pizza Dough, 103
Polpotte, 123
Pork Bits, 129
Pork-Clam Balls, 123
Pork Pastry Rolls, 104
Pork Pâté, 76
Pork Sui Mi, 166
Port-Cheddar Spread, 29
Potato Bread, 23
Pot Stickers (Kuo-Tieh), 169
Potted Shrimp, 31
Poultry Stock, 13
Prawns Stuffed with Clams, 95
Puff Pastry, Quick, 102
Puff Pastry Fingers, 105
Puff Pastry Squares, 105
Pumpkin Bread, 25

Quiches, 116
  Asparagus, 117
  Cheese, 116
  Crab, 119
  Green Tomato, 117
  Mushroom, 118
  Spinach, 118
  Zucchini, 119

Raclette, 133
Raw Vegetable Platter, 148
Rillettes, 77

Roast Beef Platter, 162
Roast Pig, 176
Rolled Sandwiches, 34
Roll-ups, 47
  Cheese, 47
  Lox, 48
Roquefort Cookies, 178
Rumaki, 62

Salads
  Celeriac, 150
  Sunchoke, 149
  Tabooleh, 36
Salmon Spread, 28
Salmon, Poached Whole, 158
Sandwiches
  Peta, 35
  Pinwheel, 34
  Rolled, 34
  Stacked, 34
Sao Pai Gut (Barbecued Spareribs), 173
Sashimi, 51
Sauces and Dressings
  Anchovy, 10
  Béarnaise, 7
  Boiled or Cream Dressing, 11
  Bordelaise, 9
  Chutney, 9
  Curry, 8
  French Dressing, 11
  Herb, 9
  Hollandaise, 7
  Horseradish, 10
  Mayonnaises, 6
  Mornay, 8
  Mousseline, 8
  Mushroom Duxelle, 12
  Orange Dressing, 150
  Sour Cream Dill, 11

Tomato, 10
Tomato-Ham Duxelle, 12
Velouté, 8
Vinaigrette, 10
Whiskey, 8
Yoghurt, 11
Sauerkraut Balls, 124
Sausages Wrapped in Pastry, 106
Seafood Cocktail, 92
Seviche, 153
Short Crust Pastry, 102
Shrimp and Artichokes, 130
Shrimp Balls, 61
Shrimp Balls, Deep-Fried, 122
Shrimp Bowl, 49
Shrimp, Broiled Marinated, 64
Shrimp Pasties, 107
Shrimp, Potted, 31
Shrimp Sauce on Toast, 99
Shrimp, Stuffed, 52
Shrimp Triangles, Deep-Fried, 65
Sin Sul Lo, Korean, 137
Snail Canape, 95
Sorrel Soup, 88
Soups
  Apple Butter, 91
  Cheese-Beer, 91
  Cucumber, 89
  Herb, Chilled, 90
  Lettuce, 87
  Pea, 90
  Sorrel, 88
  Sunchoke, 89
  Tomato, Clear, 88
Sour Cream Dill Sauce, 11
Sour Cream Pastry, 102
Spinach Dip, 67
Spinach Filling for Phyllo, 113
Spinach Pie, 96
Spinach Quiche, 118

Spreads, 32-33
  Avocado Butter, 28
  Butters, Seasoned, 27
  Cottage Cheese, 30
  Eggplant, 28
  Lemon Curd, 30
  Port-Cheddar, 29
  Potted Shrimp, 31
  Salmon, 28
  Swiss Cheese, 31
Spreads and Fillings, 32-33
Stacked Sandwiches, 34
Steak Tartare, 160
Steaming, 165
Stock Jelly, 17
Stocks
  Clarifying, 13
  Fish, 13
  Poultry, Game, Meat, 13
  Vegetable, 13
Strawberries for Buffet, 179
Sunchoke Salad, 149
Sunchoke Soup, 89
Sushi, 58-59
Sweetbreads, Creamed, 127
Sweetbreads, How to Cook, 127
Sweet and Sour Sauce, 173
Sweet-Sour Meatballs, 125
Swiss Cheese Spread, 31

Tabooleh Salad, 36
Tarts, Small, 120
Tea Eggs, 174
Tepenade Sauce with Eggs, 155
Terrine of Pork, 80
Tiropetes (Feta Cheese-Filled Phyllo), 114
Toast Cups, 66
Tomato-Cheese Rounds, 43
Tomato Custard Molds, 94

Tomato-Ham Duxelle, 12
Tomato Jelly, 17
Tomato Sauce, 10
Tomato Soup, Clear, 88
Tomatoes, Stuffed, 93
Tomatoes, Stuffed Cherry, 53
Trigona (Phyllo Dessert Triangles), 183
Tuna Mousse, 159
Tuna Pâté, 76
Turkey Galantine, 82-83
Turnip Pudding (Law Pak Go), 171

Veal Filling for Phyllo, 115
Veal Galantine, 85
Vegetable Flowers, 14
Vegetable Jelly, 17
Vegetable Stock, 13
Vegetables, Marinated, 148
Vegetables, Pickled, 148
Vegetable Platter, Raw, 148
Velouté Sauce, 8
Vinaigrette Sauce, 10

Walnut Torte, Russian, 183
Watercress Cream Mold, 149
Wheat Starch Skins, 170
Whiskey Sauce, 8
Whole Wheat/Rye Bread, 24
Wonton Skins, 165
Wontons, Fried, 168

Yakitori, 145
Yoghurt Sauce, 11

Zucchini Dip, 68
Zucchini Quiche, 119
Zucchini-Swiss Chard Frittata, 155
Zwiebelkuchen (Onion Pie), 154

biographical data

CORALIE CASTLE

Although this is Coralie Castle's third cookbook for 101 Productions, it is actually the first book she intended to write. For years the hors d'oeuvre at her own parties and those she catered in Marin County caused friends and acquaintances to beg recipes. Instead she first wrote *Soup* (1971) and followed this with *Peasant Cooking of Many Lands* (1972) in a co-authorship with Margaret Gin. In addition to her own vast collection of hors d'oeuvre, Mrs. Castle developed many new recipes for this book from ideas she gathered during two trips to Europe in the past year. Coralie Castle and her husband Alfred live in San Rafael, where they grow many of their own herbs, fruits and vegetables. Her fourth book for 101 Productions will be published in 1974.

BARBARA LAWRENCE

Barbara Lawrence is well known to San Francisco Bay Area epicures for her cooking lectures, demonstrations and articles. She was formerly dining-in columnist for *San Francisco Magazine* and food editor for Review Publications who ran her columns in five Alameda County daily newspapers. For these she received the Vesta award for writing from the American Meat Institute in 1970. Mrs. Lawrence presently writes a food column in a subscription newsletter, *Share the Wealth*, and is women's editor for the national camping magazine, *Camper Coachman*. Her first book, *Fisherman's Wharf Cookbook*, was published in 1971 by Nitty Gritty Productions. She and her husband, Robert, operate Lawrence's Ltd., a gourmet cookware store in Castro Valley, California.

KAREN LYNCH

Karen Lynch works as a free-lance graphic designer, but her artistic talents are equally at home in the world of fine arts. She received her degree in fine arts from the Ringling School of Art in Sarasota, Florida. Her paintings, collages and etchings as well as her graphic designs have been exhibited in 10 group shows, mostly at galleries in the Northeastern United States, and in two one-man shows: The Exit Gallery, operated by Yale University in New Haven, and the Gallery Louisa in Grand Rapids, Michigan. She has also illustrated and written a book on the folklore of egg decoration which will be published by Troubador Press.